W9-BRE-031

 BREAKFAST FOR DINNER

BREAKFAST *for* DINNER

Recipes for Frittata Florentine, Huevos Rancheros, Sunny-Side-Up Burgers, and More!

★ by Lindsay Landis & Taylor Hackbarth ★

QUIRK BOOKS
PHILADELPHIA

© 2013 by Lindsay Landis and Taylor Hackbarth

All rights reserved. No part of this book may be reproduced in any
form without written permission from the publisher.

Library of Congress Cataloging in Publication Number: 2012904031

ISBN: 978-1-59474-613-0

Printed in China
Typeset in DIN, Eames Century Modern, and Helvetica Neue
Designed by Katie Hatz
Production management by John J. McGurk

Quirk Books
215 Church St.
Philadelphia, PA 19106
quirkbooks.com

10 9 8 7 6 5 4 3 2 1

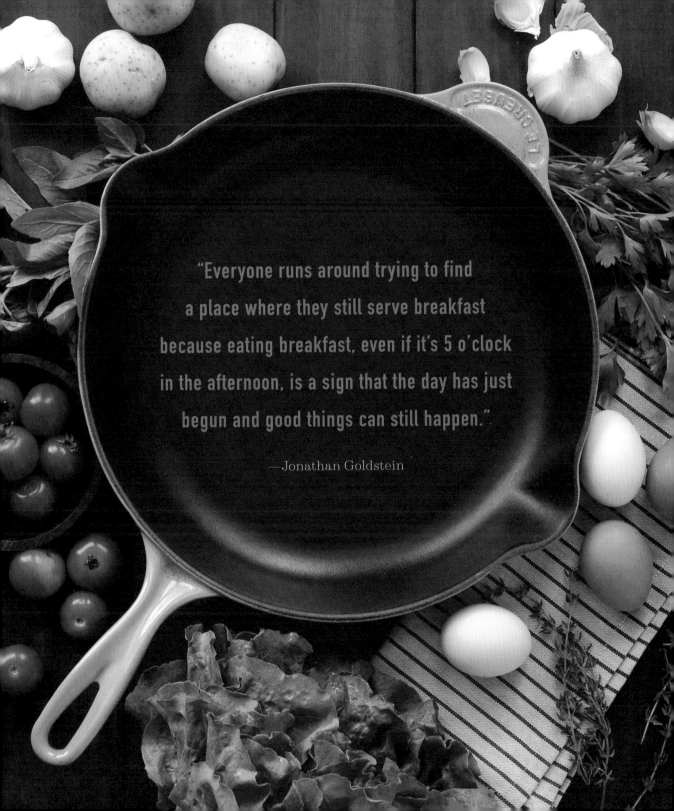

"Everyone runs around trying to find a place where they still serve breakfast because eating breakfast, even if it's 5 o'clock in the afternoon, is a sign that the day has just begun and good things can still happen."

—Jonathan Goldstein

CONTENTS

INTRODUCTION

Breakfast for dinner isn't anything new. We've all enjoyed it. From a quick supper of pancakes smothered with maple syrup to a late-night bowl of cereal, breakfast dishes at dinnertime are quite possibly the ultimate in comfort food.

We both have fond childhood memories of those special nights when waffles or French toast appeared on the dinner table. To us, it was such a treat. In reality, our parents were probably short on time or had only a few random ingredients in the fridge, making do with what was on hand.

The truth is, most people don't have time in the morning to take advantage of all the amazing flavors traditionally associated with breakfast. Which is why breakfast for dinner is such a perfect way to enjoy your morning favorites when time isn't as much of an issue.

Throughout this book, we've given typical breakfast dishes a twist and infused morning flavors into more customary evening preparations. While some dishes may be instantly recognizable as wake-up foods, others have subtler ties to the first meal of the day: a hint of grapefruit shining brightly in a rich and creamy risotto, for example, or a robust undertone of coffee in a hearty pot of baked beans. We love these flavors, so why not enjoy them at dinnertime, too? After all, they say breakfast is the most important meal of the day—whether it's served in the morning, afternoon, or middle of the night.

GETTING STARTED

Here's the beauty of breakfast for dinner: you know you can make it when all else fails. It's so much more satisfying than takeout Chinese. And the ingredients aren't fussy or hard to find. If you have a handle on the basics, you're good to go.

Bacon

Thick or thin, smoked or cured, it's all about personal preference. With the exception of the Bacon Old-Fashioned (page 119), for which a smoky bacon is necessary for flavoring the drink, use whatever kind of bacon you like best.

Butter

We prefer to use unsalted butter in our cooking because it lets us control the amount of salt. If all you have is salted butter, reduce the salt by $\frac{1}{4}$ teaspoon per stick of butter.

Eggs

Large eggs are called for in most of the recipes in this book, but medium eggs are ideal when they're to sit atop something else, like the Sunny-Side-Up Burgers (page 62). Our preference is always for farm-fresh eggs. The yolks are a deep golden color, the trademark of a true pastured egg. (Supermarket eggs tend to have lighter yolks, the result of the chickens' grain-based diets.) When it comes to eggs, fresher is always better, with one exception: for hard-boiling, older white eggs are easier to peel.

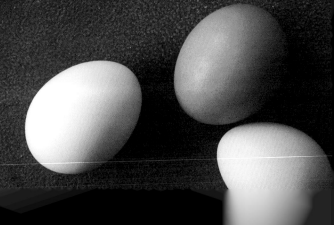

Milk

Heavy cream, half-and-half, whole, 2 percent, skim—the only difference is the fat content. We don't advise swapping one for another, especially in baking recipes, because the results may not be what you expect. Buttermilk is a different product altogether, so don't confuse it with other dairy milks. However, if you don't have buttermilk on hand for a recipe, you can easily make your own. Just add a splash of lemon juice to whole milk and let it sour for 5 or 10 minutes.

Flour

All-purpose flour is just that: good for all purposes, such as breads, cookies, and pancakes. A few recipes (such as the Biscuit Waffles on page 65) call for self-rising flour, which produces a particularly flaky biscuit. You can use all-purpose, cup for cup, in its place, plus 1 teaspoon baking powder and 1/4 teaspoon salt per cup of flour.

Olive Oil

Because olive oil has a relatively low smoke point (the temperature at which it begins to break down), the flavor can become unpleasant when it is heated to high temperatures. For high-heat cooking or frying, use canola or peanut oil instead.

Salt

Our favorite all-purpose type is kosher salt; it's what we use daily in our kitchen and what we've used for all the recipes in this book. Iodized table salt may be slightly saltier, so adjust to taste if that's what you're using.

Produce

You'll find all sorts of fruits and veggies in the recipes that follow. They're easily interchangeable to suit seasonality and personal taste. Swap broccoli for peas and carrots. Replace blueberries with raspberries, blackberries, or fresh sliced peaches. It's hard to go wrong with anything that's in season!

MAIN DISHES

a fancy brunch classic

STEAK & EGGS BENEDICT

makes 4 servings ★ total time: 45 minutes

A hearty rib-eye steak takes the place of ham in a dish that's as delicious for dinner as it is for brunch. Replacing the lemon juice in the hollandaise sauce with white balsamic vinegar is a subtle substitution that complements the steak and poached eggs perfectly.

For Poached Eggs

3 tablespoons distilled white vinegar

8 large eggs

For Steaks

1 tablespoon canola oil

2 (8-ounce) rib-eye steaks, at room temperature

Pinch salt and black pepper

For Hollandaise Sauce

2 large egg yolks

Pinch kosher salt

1/2 cup (1 stick) unsalted butter, melted and cooled to lukewarm

1 tablespoon white balsamic vinegar*

1/8 teaspoon ground cayenne pepper, plus more for topping

4 English muffins, halved and lightly toasted

Freshly ground black pepper

1/2 teaspoon chopped fresh chives (optional)

* White balsamic vinegar is similar in flavor to regular balsamic but is light in color. If you can't find it, use white wine vinegar instead.

1. For poached eggs (see poaching tips, page 16), crack 1 egg into a small ramekin. Fill a saucepan with water to a depth of 2 inches. Add white vinegar and bring to a bare simmer over medium heat. Add egg and cook for 3 1/2 to 4 minutes, or until it is roughly 30 seconds shy of being done to your liking. Lift egg out of pan with a slotted spoon and transfer to a plate. Repeat with remaining eggs. Keep water at a simmer; you will use it to warm the eggs just prior to serving.

2. Heat oil in a large, heavy skillet over medium-high heat. Season both sides of steaks with salt and pepper. Cook steaks for 3 to 4 minutes per side depending on thickness and desired doneness. Transfer to a cutting board and tent with foil; let steaks rest for 5 to 10 minutes.

3. To prepare hollandaise, whisk together egg yolks, salt, and 1 teaspoon water in a glass or stainless-steel heatproof bowl. Set bowl over a pan of gently simmering water (make sure the bowl doesn't touch the water), and whisk constantly until mixture thickens. Slowly drizzle in melted butter, whisking vigorously. Whisk in vinegar, a little at a time, followed by cayenne pepper.

4. Return eggs to simmering water for 20 seconds, or until hot. Slice steaks crosswise against the grain. Arrange slices in a single layer on toasted muffins; top with poached eggs. Drizzle hollandaise sauce over eggs; top with black pepper, cayenne pepper, and chives, if desired, and serve.

★ ★ ★

More to Try

★ **Nova Lox Benedict:** Replace steak with thin slices of Nova lox.

★ **Thanksgiving Benedict:** Top muffins with slices of roasted turkey breast and a dollop of cranberry sauce.

★ **Veggie Benedict:** Make it meatless with sautéed spinach, asparagus, and/or artichoke hearts on top of a thick slice of tomato.

PERFECTLY POACHED EGGS

To poach eggs, you cook them in gently simmering water. It's a notoriously tricky task that may take a bit of practice to master. But have no fear: there's more than one way to poach an egg. Here are our three favorites. *Makes 1 egg. Time: 1 to 6 minutes.*

1. Whirlpool: Crack 1 egg into a small dish. Fill a saucepan with water to a depth of 2 inches. Add 3 tablespoons of distilled white vinegar and bring to a bare simmer over medium heat. When small bubbles coat the bottom of the pan, stir water in a circular pattern, forming a whirlpool in the center. Stop stirring and carefully pour egg into whirlpool. Cook for 4½ to 5 minutes, or until white is cooked but yolk is still jiggly. For a firmer yolk, cook for about 30 seconds more. Carefully remove egg with a slotted spoon.

2. Poaching Cups: Silicone poaching cups are a handy tool for poaching multiple eggs at once. Lightly grease the cups, crack an egg into each one, and then place them in a pot of simmering water. Cover and cook for 5 to 6 minutes or more to achieve desired doneness. Remove cups from pot using a slotted spoon; turn cups inside out to remove eggs.

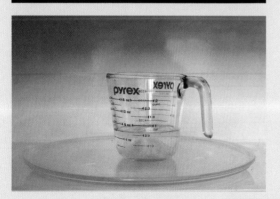

3. Microwave: Crack 1 egg into a glass measuring cup and add ½ cup water and a splash of distilled white vinegar. Microwave on high power for 45 seconds or more to achieve desired doneness. Remove with a slotted spoon. Microwaves vary, so adjust the cooking time to suit your model.

PITA BREAD

Once you've made pita bread from scratch, you'll never want to buy it again. A seemingly simple dough puffs like magic into soft, pillowy pockets that are perfect for dipping, dredging, or stuffing with your favorite fillings. *Makes about 10 to 12 pitas. Active time: 1 hour. Total time: 3 hours.*

1 package (2¼ teaspoons) instant yeast

3 cups all-purpose flour, plus more as needed

1½ teaspoons salt

1 teaspoon granulated sugar

Extra-virgin olive oil, as needed

Breakfast Pitas

Fill fresh pitas with your favorite scrambled eggs or breakfast hash.

1. Place 1½ cups lukewarm water in a large mixing bowl. Sprinkle yeast over water and stir until dissolved. Let sit for 5 minutes, or until foamy. Add flour, salt, and sugar and stir with wooden spoon until dough comes together.

2. Turn out dough onto a floured surface and knead for 10 minutes, or until dough is smooth and elastic, adding more flour as needed to prevent dough from sticking to the work surface.

3. Place dough ball in a large bowl that has been coated with a thin layer of olive oil; turn dough to coat it in oil. Loosely cover and let rise in a warm spot for 1 to 2 hours, or until doubled in size.

4. Preheat oven to 500°F. Place a baking stone or large baking sheet on a rack in the bottom third of your oven.

5. Divide dough into 10 to 12 equal pieces; flatten each piece slightly with your hands and arrange in a single layer on a floured surface or baking sheet. Cover with a clean dishcloth and let sit for 10 minutes.

6. On a lightly floured surface, roll out each piece of dough into a 5- to 6-inch circle approximately ¼ inch thick.

7. Place 2 rounds at a time onto preheated baking stone or baking sheet; bake for about 4 minutes, or until the bread balloons. (If your bread doesn't puff every time, don't worry. It doesn't always work perfectly, but the bread will still taste just as good.) Using a spatula or heatproof tongs, flip and bake for 2 minutes more, or until lightly golden.

8. Transfer to a cooling rack for 5 minutes, then place in plastic storage bags or wrap with a clean kitchen towel (to keep the bread soft). Pita bread can be stored for up to a week in a zip-top bag in the refrigerator or up to a month in the freezer.

EASY MARINARA

Marinara sauce doesn't always have to come from a jar. This simple version is quick to make and puts jarred sauce to shame. *Makes about 2 cups. Total time: 30 minutes.*

2 tablespoons extra-virgin olive oil

½ medium yellow onion, chopped

2 garlic cloves, minced

1 (15-ounce) can diced tomatoes, with their juices

1 tablespoon chopped fresh or 1 teaspoon dried basil

2 teaspoons chopped fresh or ¼ teaspoon dried oregano

¼ teaspoon salt

¼ teaspoon pepper

Heat oil in a medium saucepan over medium heat. Add onions and cook until softened, about 3 minutes. Stir in garlic and cook for 1 minute more. Add tomatoes with their juices, ¼ cup water, herbs, salt, and pepper; simmer for about 20 minutes, stirring occasionally, or until tomatoes begin to break down and sauce starts to thicken.

an avocado lover's new best friend

AVOCADO CREAM SAUCE

This cool and creamy sauce is the perfect accompaniment to anything spicy. Use it in place of sour cream or guacamole in your favorite Mexican-style dishes (like the burritos on page 25), or even as a dip for tortilla chips. *Makes 1 cup. Total time: 5 minutes.*

- 1 large avocado, pitted and cut into chunks
- Juice of 1 lime
- 1/4 cup sour cream
- 1/4 cup whole milk
- Salt, to taste

In a blender or food processor, blend avocado, lime juice, sour cream, and milk on high speed until creamy. Season to taste with salt.

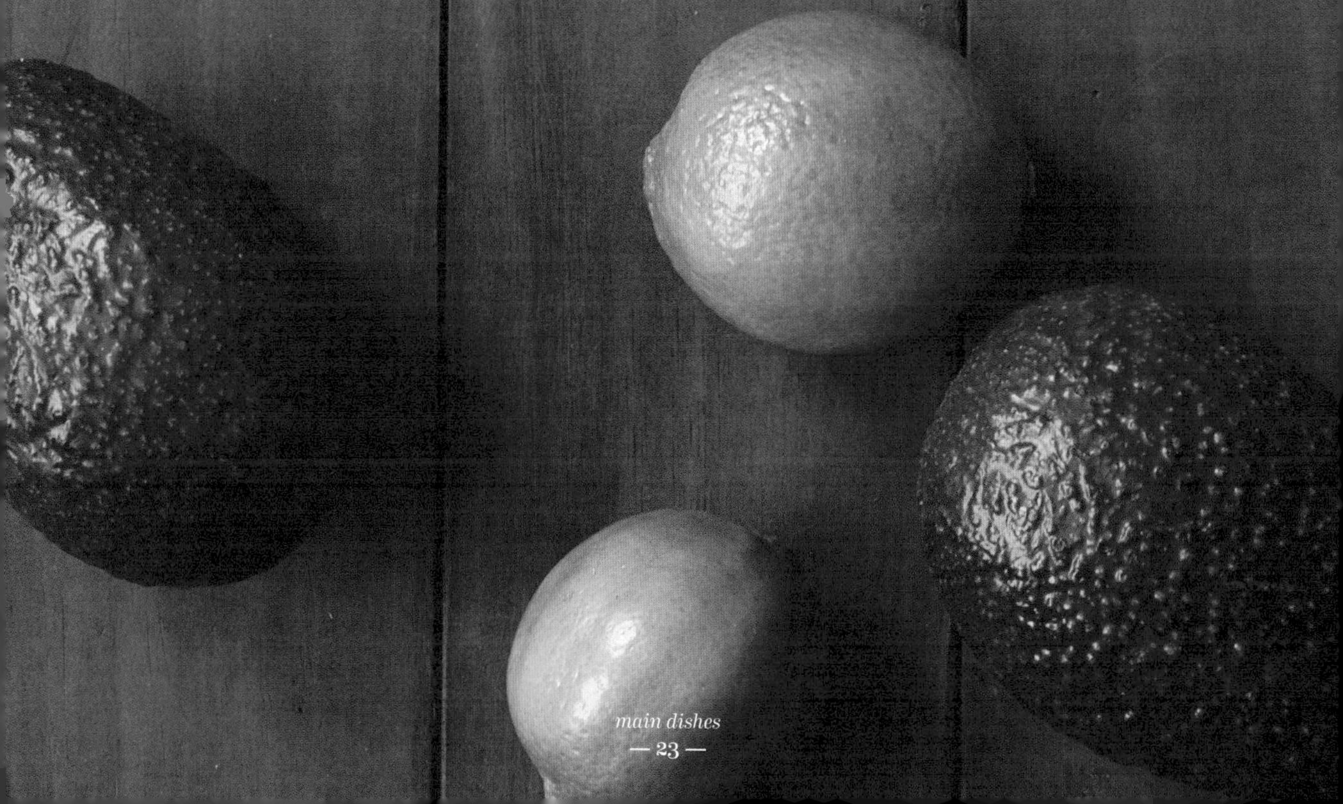

with spinach, sweet potatoes, and avocado cream

EGG & CHORIZO BURRITOS

makes 4 burritos ★ total time: 35 minutes

Breakfast burritos have been done before, but not like this. Our breakfast-gone-dinner burrito is anything but cliché, with a spicy chorizo, spinach, and sweet potato filling enrobed in a thin, crepe-like layer of egg, finished with fresh Avocado Cream Sauce and wrapped in a flour tortilla.

4 10-inch flour tortillas

For Filling
4 ounces dry-cured chorizo,* casings removed, chopped into ¼-inch cubes

¼ medium yellow onion, chopped

1 sweet potato, chopped into ¼-inch cubes (about 1 cup, chopped)

8 ounces frozen spinach, thawed and chopped (about 1 cup)

For Eggs
2 tablespoons unsalted butter, divided

4 large eggs

For Topping
½ cup Avocado Cream Sauce (page 23)

*The dry-cured, or Spanish-style, chorizo called for in this recipe can be hard to find, but you can substitute 8 ounces of fresh, or Mexican-style, chorizo: cook over medium-high heat, stirring and breaking up any large chunks as you go, about 5 to 7 minutes, before adding onion in step 2.

1. Preheat oven to 250°F. Stack tortillas, wrap in aluminum foil, place on a baking sheet, and bake for 15 to 20 minutes, or until heated through.

2. To prepare the filling, heat a large skillet over medium-high heat. Cook chorizo until it begins to brown and much of the fat has been rendered, 5 to 7 minutes. Stir in onions and cook until translucent, about 2 minutes more. Reduce heat to medium and stir in sweet potatoes; cook until just tender, about 10 minutes. Stir in spinach and cook until heated through.

3. Melt ½ tablespoon butter in an 8-inch nonstick skillet over medium heat. In a small bowl, whisk 1 egg until pale yellow. Add egg to hot skillet and swirl around the pan to form an even layer. Cover and cook about 1 minute, or until cooked through. Gently slide onto 1 tortilla; return to baking sheet in oven to keep warm. Repeat with remaining eggs and tortillas, adding more butter to pan as needed.

4. Spoon one-fourth of the filling down the center of each tortilla. Drizzle with Avocado Cream Sauce. Roll up and serve.

➤ FRITTATA FLORENTINE ➤

makes 4 to 6 servings ★ active time: 45 minutes ★ total time: 1 hour

Frittatas, like their eggy cousins quiches and omelets, are open to endless possibilities. This quick and easy recipe combines a fluffy egg base with spinach, Parmesan, and goat cheese; but the beauty of it is that you can use whatever meats, veggies, or cheeses you happen to have on hand.

8 large eggs

1 cup half-and-half

½ cup (about 2 ounces) shredded Parmesan cheese, divided

¼ teaspoon grated nutmeg

¼ teaspoon ground cayenne pepper

Salt and black pepper, to taste

1 tablespoon extra-virgin olive oil

1 medium yellow onion, diced

1 garlic clove, minced

10 ounces frozen spinach,* thawed and chopped

¼ cup (2 ounces) goat cheese

*Fresh spinach works just as well here; just rinse and coarsely chop it and then cook until wilted.

1. Preheat oven to 400°F. In a large bowl, whisk together eggs, half-and-half, ¼ cup of the Parmesan, nutmeg, cayenne, salt, and black pepper.

2. Heat oil in a heavy ovenproof 12-inch skillet over medium heat. Add onions and cook until translucent, about 4 minutes. Stir in garlic and spinach and cook until fragrant, 1 to 2 minutes more. Gently fold in egg mixture. Cook until partially set, about 3 to 5 minutes. Sprinkle goat cheese and remaining Parmesan cheese over top.

3. Place pan in oven and bake until frittata is puffed and golden, about 15 to 20 minutes. Let cool slightly, then cut into wedges and serve.

★ ★ ★

Flavor Inspirations

Take the opportunity to empty your fridge of leftovers and try these tasty variations, or make up one of your own:

★ **Potato & Country Ham Frittata,** with red potato and cubed ham or bacon

★ **Garden Veggie Frittata,** with freshly chopped asparagus, mushrooms, peas, and carrots

★ **Broccoli Garlic Frittata,** with extra garlic, broccoli, and Gruyère cheese

★ **Greek Frittata,** with zucchini, olives, sun-dried tomatoes, and feta

simple and satisfying, Southern and Spanish

ANDOUILLE SHRIMP & GRITS

makes 4 servings ★ active time: 45 minutes ★ total time: 1 hour

Shrimp and grits is a classic Southern favorite, often served for breakfast, dinner, or any meal in between. This version includes a saffron-infused squash and andouille sausage hash reminiscent of paella and is served with crispy kale chips and creamy goat cheese.

For Grits

1 cup stone-ground white grits (not instant)

1/3 cup goat cheese, plus more for topping

1/2 cup heavy cream

Salt and black pepper, to taste

For Hash

1 pinch saffron threads*

4 ounces andouille sausage, cut into 3/8-inch cubes (about 1 cup cubed)

Olive oil, for pan (if needed)

1 pound shrimp, peeled and deveined

1 pound butternut squash, cut into cubes (about 2 cups cubed)

1 teaspoon paprika

Store-bought or homemade kale chips (see page 30)

*Saffron is not cheap, but a little goes a long way. Look for it in the spice aisle of the grocery store. There's really no substitute in terms of flavor, so if you can't find it, simply leave it out.

1. Bring 3 cups water to a simmer in a large saucepan. Gradually whisk in grits. Reduce heat to low. Gently simmer, stirring often and adding water 1/4 cup at a time as needed, about 45 minutes to 1 hour or until tender (the consistency of the grits is a matter of personal preference, but if they appear thick and pasty, add a little water). Stir in goat cheese and cream. Season to taste with salt and pepper. Cover and keep warm.

2. For the hash, soak saffron threads in 1 tablespoon warm water; set aside. Heat a large skillet over medium-high heat. Add sausage and cook until crispy, about 10 minutes; transfer to a bowl with a slotted spoon. Return skillet to medium-high heat. If skillet seems dry, add a splash of olive oil. Cook shrimp until just opaque, 2 to 3 minutes. Transfer to bowl with sausage. Add squash to skillet and cook over medium-high heat until tender, 3 to 5 minutes. Stir in cooked sausage and shrimp, along with saffron mixture and paprika. Cook until liquid is thickened and shrimp is heated through. Season to taste with salt and pepper.

3. Spoon warm grits into bowls. Top with sausage-and-shrimp hash, crumbled goat cheese, and kale chips, and serve.

★ ★ ★

Spicy and heavily smoked, andouille is pork sausage popular in Cajun cuisine. Look for "hot links" or "Cajun-style" sausage in your grocery store—if you can stand the heat!

KALE CHIPS

Kale chips are something of a culinary miracle: a harsh, bitter green becomes a paper-thin "chip" that melts in your mouth. The key to making these snacks extra crispy is drying them completely before baking; We give them a vigorous spin-dry in a salad spinner and then lay them out on paper towels until not a drop of moisture remains. Kale chips are best enjoyed right out of the oven. *Makes 4 servings. Total time: 10 minutes.*

2 large handfuls fresh kale leaves, rinsed and thoroughly dried

2 tablespoons extra-virgin olive oil

Fine sea salt, to taste

Preheat oven 400°F. Remove and discard large veins from kale and cut leaves into 2-inch pieces. Toss with oil and spread in a single layer on two foil-lined baking sheets. Bake for 5 to 7 minutes or until crispy, taking care not to let the leaves brown. Toss with salt and serve.

BUTTERMILK RANCH SAUCE

This thick and creamy buttermilk ranch dipping sauce is the perfect compliment to Cornflake-Crusted Chicken Tenders (page 32), but would also be a great sauce for fish or french fries. *Makes ½ cup. Total time: 10 minutes.*

⅓ cup mayonnaise

¼ cup buttermilk, plus more as needed

1 garlic clove, minced, or ¼ teaspoon garlic powder

2 tablespoons chopped fresh chives

1 teaspoon chopped fresh or ¼ teaspoon dried dill

Salt and black pepper, to taste

In a small bowl, whisk together mayonnaise and buttermilk until smooth. Add more buttermilk as needed to achieve desired onsistency. Stir in garlic, chives, and dill. Season to taste with salt and pepper.

cornflakes: a chef's secret

CORNFLAKE-CRUSTED CHICKEN TENDERS

makes 4 servings ★ active time: 30 minutes ★ total time: 45 minutes

The beloved breakfast cereal gives this kids' menu staple a bit of a makeover and takes it to new, crunchy, flavorful heights.

For Chicken

½ cup all-purpose flour

¾ teaspoon salt

½ teaspoon pepper

2 large eggs

4 cups cornflakes, finely crushed (about 1 cup crushed)

2 teaspoons dried parsley

1 teaspoon garlic powder

1 teaspoon dried dill

1½ pounds boneless skinless chicken tenders (about 20 tenders)

For Dipping

½ cup store-bought ranch dressing or Buttermilk Ranch Sauce (page 31)

1. Preheat oven to 400°F. Cover a baking sheet with aluminum foil and set a heatproof wire baking rack on top; spray rack lightly with cooking spray.

2. In a small bowl or shallow dish, season flour with ¼ teaspoon each salt and pepper; whisk eggs in another shallow dish. In a third shallow dish, mix cornflakes with parsley, garlic, dill, the remaining ½ teaspoon salt, and the remaining ¼ teaspoon of pepper.

3. Dredge chicken in flour to coat, shaking off excess. Dip into egg and then into cornflake mixture, making sure entire surface is coated. Arrange on prepared baking rack.

4. Bake for 12 to 15 minutes, or until golden brown and cooked through, flipping once during cooking. Serve with Buttermilk Ranch Sauce for dipping.

★ ★ ★

A Frugal Trick

If you can't find or don't want to spend the extra money on chicken tenders, simply place a whole chicken breast between two layers of plastic wrap, pound it to an even ½-inch thickness, and slice it into strips.

GREEK BAKED EGGS

makes 4 servings ★ total time: 20 minutes

Baked eggs—often called shirred eggs or, if you're French, *oeufs en cocotte*—come out of the oven in record time with a creamy, custardlike consistency that you just can't achieve through frying. We top them with a Greek-inspired combination of olives, sun-dried tomatoes, herbs, and feta cheese.

¼ cup heavy cream

¼ cup (½ stick) unsalted butter

8 eggs

⅓ cup chopped kalamata olives

¼ cup flat-leaf parsley, chopped

2 tablespoons chopped fresh oregano

¼ cup chopped sun-dried tomatoes

¼ cup crumbled feta cheese

Pinch freshly ground black pepper

Flaked or coarse sea salt, to taste (optional)

1. Place 8 small or 4 medium ramekins on a baking sheet and place in oven. Preheat oven to 375°F. Divide butter and cream among hot ramekins (small ramekins will get ½ tablespoon of each and larger, 2-egg ramekins will get 1 tablespoon). Return to oven until butter is melted and sizzling.

2. Remove ramekins from oven and crack eggs into them. Return to oven and bake until whites are set (yolks may appear slightly underdone), 7 to 10 minutes, or longer if you use larger ramekins or prefer a firmer yolk. Top with olives, herbs, sun-dried tomatoes, and feta cheese and bake for 1 minute more. Season with pepper and finish with a sprinkling of sea salt, if desired. Serve.

★ ★ ★

Baked Eggs for a Crowd

Whether you're feeding two or twenty-two, baked eggs are easy. For larger crowds, you can increase this recipe and bake eggs all together in a large ovenproof pan or casserole. Use ½ tablespoon each of butter and cream per egg and adjust cooking time accordingly.

Taylor's favorite

⫸ BACON FRIED RICE ⫷

makes 4 to 6 servings ★ active time: 45 minutes ★ total time: 1 hour 30 minutes

Fried rice is one of those side dishes that never gets the credit it deserves. We think it's time it took center stage. Tossed with smoky bacon, scrambled eggs, and green peas, it's a sure crowd-pleaser. Chopsticks optional.

2 cups brown jasmine rice*

6 slices bacon (about ½ pound), diced

½ large yellow onion, thinly sliced

4 green onions, thinly sliced, plus more for topping

1½ tablespoons minced garlic (from 3 large cloves)

1 tablespoon finely minced ginger (from a 1-inch piece)

1 cup frozen peas

4 large eggs, beaten

2 tablespoons vegetable oil

3 tablespoons soy sauce, or to taste

½ teaspoon sriracha, or to taste

1 carrot, thinly sliced or ribboned using a vegetable peeler, for topping

*Brown jasmine rice is our favorite for this recipe; its long grains and outer hull (something that white jasmine rice lacks) give it the perfect texture for frying. If substituting white jasmine rice, follow the cooking directions on the package, but use slightly less water and cook it until it's just barely done.

1. In a saucepan over medium-high heat, bring rice and 3 cups water to a boil. Cover and reduce heat to low. Simmer for 20 to 30 minutes, or until rice is just tender but still has a slight bite; drain any remaining water. Fluff with a fork. Cover and let cool for at least 30 minutes, or refrigerate overnight.

2. In a large nonstick skillet or wok over medium-high heat, cook bacon until it is browned and fat is rendered, about 10 minutes. Drain any excess fat from pan (you still want a thin layer coating the bottom) and push bacon to sides of pan. In the center, add onions and cook until softened, about 2 minutes. Stir in green onions, garlic, and ginger and cook for 3 minutes, taking care not to let the garlic brown. Stir in peas and cook for 2 minutes, or until warm. Transfer mixture to a medium bowl.

3. Lower heat to medium, add eggs, and scramble for 2 to 3 minutes, or until fully cooked. Add eggs to bacon mixture. Wipe out skillet (carefully, as it may be hot), add vegetable oil, and return to medium-high heat. When oil is hot but not smoking, add cooked rice and spread in an even layer. Cook, stirring occasionally, for 5 minutes, or until rice is heated through and slightly crispy. Stir in bacon–egg mixture. Season to taste with soy sauce and sriracha (if your bacon is on the salty side, you may want to use less soy sauce). Top with green onions and carrots and serve hot.

crazy delicious anytime food

⇒ LOCO MOCO ⇒

makes 2 servings ★ active time: 30 minutes ★ total time: 8 hours 30 minutes

This classic Hawaiian dish typically consists of a generous portion of white rice topped with a hamburger patty—or grilled Spam—and a sunny-side-up egg, plus lots of brown gravy. Our version takes the basic rice/meat/egg concept and elevates it with coconut-infused sticky rice, savory ground pork, and a sweet-and-salty soy sauce reduction.

For Coconut Rice

1 cup white sticky rice*

1/2 cup coconut milk

For Soy Reduction

1/4 cup low-sodium soy sauce**

2 tablespoons light brown sugar, packed

1/2 teaspoon sriracha

For Pork

1/4 pound ground pork

1/8 teaspoon salt

1/8 teaspoon black pepper

For Topping

1 teaspoon vegetable oil

2 large eggs

2 green onions, thinly sliced

2 tablespoons roughly chopped fresh cilantro

*Sold as Sho-Chiku-Bai sweet rice, or sometimes just called sweet rice, white sticky rice can be found at specialty grocers and Asian food stores. You can use sushi rice instead, though it may need more liquid and a slightly longer cooking time.

**Regular soy sauce won't work here; it makes the reduction too salty.

1. Combine rice with 1 cup cold water; cover and refrigerate for 6 to 8 hours. Pour rice and any remaining liquid into a saucepan. Stir in coconut milk and bring to a boil over medium heat. Cover and reduce heat to medium-low; simmer for 10 minutes, or until rice is tender and liquid is absorbed. Remove from heat; keep covered and let stand for at least 5 minutes.

2. In a small saucepan, combine soy sauce, 2 tablespoons water, brown sugar, and sriracha. Simmer over medium heat, stirring occasionally, until thickened and reduced by half, 6 to 8 minutes.

3. Heat a large nonstick skillet over medium-high heat. Add pork and season lightly with salt and pepper. Cook, breaking it up with a wooden spoon, until it begins to brown, about 7 to 9 minutes. Transfer to a bowl and cover with aluminum foil to keep warm.

4. Carefully wipe out skillet (it may be hot) and return to medium heat; brush with vegetable oil. Crack eggs into opposite sides of the pan to keep them from running together. Cover and cook for 3 to 4 minutes. If you prefer firmer yolks, cook for another 1 to 2 minutes.

5. Divide rice between serving bowls. Top with ground pork and a fried egg. Drizzle with soy reduction, sprinkle green onion and cilantro on top, and serve.

the Mexican breakfast of champions

═ HUEVOS RANCHEROS TACOS ═

makes 4 servings ★ total time: 1 hour

Huevos rancheros, or ranch-style eggs, have always been one of our favorite breakfasts, combining runny eggs with corn tortillas and ranchero sauce, a cooked tomato salsa. They're even more delicious as a tasty taco.

For Ranchero Sauce

1 tablespoon extra-virgin olive oil

½ medium yellow onion, chopped

2 garlic cloves, minced

1 large jalapeño, seeded and chopped

1 (15-ounce) can fire-roasted diced tomatoes (or regular diced tomatoes)

½ cup vegetable broth

1 tablespoon chopped fresh cilantro

2 teaspoons chopped fresh oregano

1 chipotle pepper in adobo sauce, seeded and chopped, plus ½ tablespoon adobo sauce*

¼ teaspoon salt

Freshly ground black pepper, to taste

For Tacos

1 (15-ounce) can refried black beans

3 tablespoons vegetable oil, divided

8 corn tortillas

½ cup shredded cheddar or mozzarella cheese

8 large eggs

2 tablespoons chopped fresh cilantro

*Chipotle peppers are smoked jalapeños and are commonly sold canned in a spicy tomato-based marinade called adobo sauce. Look for them in the international foods aisle of your local grocery store.

1. Heat olive oil in a saucepan over medium heat. Add onions, garlic, and jalapeños and cook for 3 minutes, or until softened. Stir in tomatoes with their juices, vegetable broth, cilantro, oregano, chipotle, adobo sauce, salt, and pepper. Simmer for 20 minutes, stirring occasionally, until sauce thickens. Let cool, then process in a blender or food processor until smooth. Sauce can be made 1 day ahead and refrigerated in an airtight container; warm prior to serving.

2. Preheat oven to 350°F. Combine refried beans with ¼ cup water in a small saucepan over medium-low heat and cook, stirring, until heated through.

3. Heat 1 teaspoon of the vegetable oil in a large nonstick skillet over medium heat. Add tortillas, 2 at a time so that they do not overlap, and cook for about 1 minute per side, adding more oil as needed. Arrange in a single layer on a large baking sheet. Spread 2 tablespoons of warm beans on each tortilla; sprinkle with cheese. Place in oven and bake for 3 to 4 minutes, or until cheese is melted.

4. In the skillet you used to cook tortillas, heat ½ tablespoon of the vegetable oil over medium-high heat. Crack 4 eggs into skillet. Cover and cook for 4 minutes, or until whites are cooked and a white film begins to form over the yolk; if you prefer firmer eggs, cook for 1 minute more. Separate eggs and place 1 on each tortilla. Repeat with remaining 4 eggs. Top with ranchero sauce and freshly chopped cilantro, and serve.

The Old-Fashioned Way

For more traditional (not taco-style) huevos rancheros, top lightly crispy corn tortillas with ranchero sauce and fried eggs. Serve the beans on the side, if desired.

creamy pasta with pancetta

✦ GREEN PEA CARBONARA ✦

makes 4 servings ★ total time: 40 minutes

Tender peas cut the richness of this traditionally heavy sauce, giving it a subtle sweetness and gorgeous green hue. Splurge on good-quality pasta for this recipe; artisan pasta that has been extruded through a brass die has a unique surface texture, with plenty of nooks and crannies for the sauce to explore.

1½ cups frozen peas, thawed

1 large egg*

2 large egg yolks

1 ounce (¼ cup) grated Parmesan cheese, plus more for serving

¼ cup heavy cream

¼ teaspoon salt

½ teaspoon freshly ground black pepper

4 ounces pancetta or bacon, cubed

1 medium yellow onion, chopped

1 pound rigatoni

*Do note that the eggs in this recipe are not fully cooked; we recommend using farm-fresh eggs from a trusted source. Or buy pasteurized eggs if you're worried about bacteria.

1. In a blender or food processor, blend peas, egg, egg yolks, cheese, and cream on high speed until smooth, about 30 seconds. Add salt and pepper.

2. In a large skillet over medium heat, cook pancetta until browned, 6 to 8 minutes (if using bacon, cook for slightly longer or until beginning to crisp, then drain excess fat from pan). Add onions and cook until softened, another 5 minutes.

3. Cook pasta according to package directions until just tender and still firm to the bite. Drain, reserving ½ cup of the pasta water. Add pasta to skillet and toss with onions and pancetta for 1 to 2 minutes. Remove skillet from heat; stir in pea mixture, working swiftly and vigorously so egg does not scramble. If sauce is too thick, mix in reserved pasta water, a little at a time. Transfer to serving bowls and top with more Parmesan cheese. Serve.

WHOLE WHEAT CREPES

Crepes can easily be made ahead of time and reheated in the microwave or a warm oven just prior to serving. For a sweet dessert crepe recipe, see page 129. *Makes 12 crepes. Total time: 30 minutes.*

1 cup white whole wheat flour*

1 cup whole milk

2 large eggs

¼ teaspoon salt

3 tablespoons unsalted butter, melted and cooled to lukewarm

Extra-virgin olive oil, for cooking

*White whole wheat flour is lighter in color and flavor than regular whole wheat. Can't find it? Substitute all-purpose flour cup for cup.

1. Place flour, milk, eggs, and salt in a blender. Add butter and pulse until smooth, about 20 seconds. Batter should be the consistency of heavy cream. Transfer to a bowl; cover and refrigerate for 30 minutes to 1 hour.

2. Heat a 6-inch nonstick skillet over medium heat. Lightly brush skillet with olive oil. Ladle 2 to 3 tablespoons of batter into the hot pan, quickly swirling it to the edges of the pan to form a thin, even layer. Cook for 1 to 2 minutes, or until bottom is golden brown; carefully flip and cook for 30 seconds more. Transfer to a plate and repeat with remaining batter, re-oiling pan as needed.

CREPES MADE EASY

Crepes may seem fancy but they're actually fairly easy to make—and sure to impress.
Makes 1 crepe. Time: 1 to 6 minutes.

1. Prepare batter according to either the savory whole wheat recipe on page 44 or the sweet dessert recipe on page 129; either way, batter should have the consistency of heavy cream. Heat a small nonstick skillet or crepe pan over medium heat (keep in mind that the diameter of the pan will be the size of your finished crepes). When pan is hot, brush with melted butter or olive oil.

2. Ladle 2 to 3 tablespoons of batter into pan (more or less, depending on the size of your pan). With a smooth motion, swirl the pan so the batter forms an even layer. It may take a few tries before you get it right—the first crepe is rarely perfect. Cook for 1 to 2 minutes, or until bottom is lightly golden brown.

3. Run a thin flexible spatula around edges of crepe to release it from pan, then carefully flip crepe. Smaller crepes will be easier to flip than large ones. Cook for an additional 30 seconds, then transfer to a plate.

spread thick with ricotta

SAVORY LENTIL & CARROT STUFFED CREPES

makes 12 crepes (4 servings) ★ total time: 1 hour

On our honeymoon in Italy, we stumbled upon the cutest little elderly couple selling *necci*, or chestnut crepes, at an outdoor market. The crepes were simple, made from chestnut flour and filled with thick and creamy ricotta cheese. We've elected to make the dish a bit more substantial, with spiced lentils and honeyed carrots for a touch of sweetness.

For Lentils

½ cup French green lentils,* rinsed

1 bay leaf

¼ onion

1 teaspoon lemon juice

2 teaspoons extra-virgin olive oil

¼ teaspoon ground cumin

¼ teaspoon ground cinnamon

Salt and black pepper, to taste

For Honeyed Carrots

1 tablespoon olive oil

1 pound carrots, peeled, halved, and sliced into ¼-inch-thick semicircles

½ onion, chopped

3 tablespoons honey

2 teaspoons lemon juice

Salt and black pepper

12 whole wheat crepes (page 44)

½ cup whole-milk ricotta cheese

2 tablespoons chopped fresh parsley

¼ cup chopped toasted hazelnuts

*If you can't find French green lentils, you can use brown lentils and cook according to package directions.

1. Place lentils in a saucepan; cover with water by 1 to 2 inches. Add bay leaf and onion and bring to a boil over medium-high heat. Reduce heat slightly and simmer for 18 to 20 minutes, or until lentils are tender. Take care not to overcook lentils, or they will be mushy. Drain well, discarding bay leaf and onion quarter, and return to saucepan. Toss with lemon juice, olive oil, cumin, and cinnamon. Season with salt and pepper.

2. Heat oil in a skillet over medium-high heat. Add carrots and onion and cook, stirring, for 5 minutes, or until onions are soft and translucent. Add honey, lemon juice, and ¼ cup water and cook until liquid has evaporated and carrots are tender, 20 to 22 minutes more. Season with salt and pepper.

3. Spread 1 tablespoon of ricotta cheese down the center of each crepe. Top with a spoonful of lentil mixture, followed by carrots. Top with chopped parsley and hazelnuts. Roll up and serve warm.

French green, or Puy, lentils are small blue-green marbled lentils that hold their shape much better than the more common brown lentil when cooked.

egg-battered and grilled

GOAT CHEESE MONTE CRISTOS

makes 4 sandwiches ★ total time: 25 minutes

Thought to be a variation of the croque-monsieur, that French breakfast (or anytime) classic, the monte cristo sandwich first appeared in the United States in the 1950s. This original turkey, ham, and cheese sandwich was coated in an egg batter and deep-fried. We prefer ours on the lighter side: grilled instead of fried and filled with thick-cut roasted turkey, goat cheese, and pepper jelly for a bit of extra sweetness and spice.

2 large eggs

1/3 cup whole milk

1/4 teaspoon salt

8 slices bread

4 ounces goat cheese, softened

1/4 cup hot red pepper jelly*

8 thick slices roasted turkey**

2 tablespoons unsalted butter

*Red pepper jelly is a sweet and (sometimes) spicy preserve made from red bell peppers. It's typically available in the preserves section of most major grocery stores.

**Honey-roasted is our favorite variety of turkey to use in this sandwich. Go to the deli counter for this one, and ask for extra-thick slices, pretty please.

1. Whisk together eggs, milk, and salt in a small bowl. Heat a large nonstick skillet over medium heat.

2. For each sandwich, spread 2 tablespoons goat cheese onto 1 bread slice, followed by 1 tablespoon pepper jelly. Top with 2 slices of turkey and another slice of bread. Trim crusts if desired. Generously brush tops of sandwiches with egg mixture.

3. Add butter to hot skillet; when it is melted and sizzling, arrange sandwiches in the skillet, egg side down. Brush the top of each sandwich with remaining egg mixture. Cook for 3 to 4 minutes, then flip, cooking until both sides are golden brown. Cut sandwiches in half diagonally and serve.

★ ★ ★

Monte Cristos for Everyone

★ **Cheddar Monte Cristos:** Not a goat cheese lover? Try this same combo with a sharp white cheddar cheese instead.

★ **Classic Monte Cristos:** Use one slice of ham, one slice of turkey, and cheddar cheese, and serve with red currant jelly on the side.

★ **Thanksgiving Monte Cristos:** Replace the pepper jelly with jellied cranberry sauce—a combination that's perfect with Thanksgiving leftovers.

a tasty way to eat your veggies

BROCCOLI & CAULIFLOWER OMELETS

makes 2 omelets ★ *active time: 20 minutes* ★ *total time: 30 minutes*

An omelet is a hearty and satisfying meal any time of day. A mix of broccoli, cauliflower, garlic, and gooey mozzarella cheese make this version both healthy and delicious. The key to the light, airy texture? Extra egg whites.

For Filling

2 tablespoons extra-virgin olive oil, plus more for brushing

1 cup broccoli florets, cut into bite-size pieces

1 cup cauliflower florets, cut into bite-size pieces

3 garlic cloves, quartered

Salt and black pepper, to taste

For Omelets

3 large eggs, plus 2 large egg whites (or another large egg)

Pinch each salt and black pepper

1 tablespoon melted butter

½ cup (2 ounces) shredded mozzarella cheese, divided

1. Preheat oven to 450°F. Line a large baking sheet with parchment paper or aluminum foil; brush with olive oil.

2. In a large bowl, toss broccoli and cauliflower together with garlic, 2 tablespoons of olive oil, salt, and pepper. Spread in a single layer on prepared baking sheet. Roast for 11 to 13 minutes, or until vegetables are tender and just starting to brown.

3. In a large bowl, vigorously whisk eggs and egg whites for 1 to 2 minutes, or until frothy. Add salt and pepper.

4. Heat an 8- or 10-inch nonstick skillet over medium heat. Brush with melted butter; if it doesn't instantly sizzle, the pan isn't hot enough. Pour half of the egg mixture into skillet. With a heatproof spatula, quickly stir the center of the eggs for 2 to 3 seconds (as if you were making scrambled eggs). Tilt the skillet and allow any remaining liquid egg to spread out around the edges. Let cook, undisturbed, for 1 to 2 minutes, or until top is no longer runny (it should still appear slightly undercooked). Arrange half of the roasted vegetables evenly on one half of the omelet. Sprinkle ¼ cup cheese over vegetables. Using a large, thin spatula, carefully fold the plain half over the filled half. Gently slide the omelet onto a serving dish.

5. Repeat with remaining ingredients for the second omelet.

★ ★ ★

Flavorful Fillings

★ **Western Omelets:** Fill with diced ham, onions, green bell peppers, and Swiss cheese.

★ **Italian Omelets:** Try mushrooms, tomato, mozzarella, and marinara sauce.

★ **Bacon Omelets:** Bacon. Lots of bacon. And maybe some cheddar cheese.

rich, filling, and completely vegetarian

POLENTA CAKES WITH SHIITAKE MUSHROOMS

makes 8 servings ★ active time: 1 hour ★ total time: 1 hour 30 minutes

Poached eggs perched atop a crisp polenta cake with an herb and mushroom topping make a perfectly satisfying meatless meal. A generous drizzle of a sweet and sticky balsamic reduction doesn't hurt, either.

For Polenta Cakes
8 ounces instant polenta*

Salt and black pepper, to taste

2 tablespoons extra-virgin olive oil

For Balsamic Reduction
½ cup balsamic vinegar

2 tablespoons light brown sugar, packed

For Shiitake Topping
4 tablespoons unsalted butter

½ cup chopped shallots

8 ounces shiitake mushrooms, stems removed and caps thinly sliced (about 4 cups stemmed and sliced)

2 teaspoons chopped fresh oregano

2 teaspoons chopped fresh thyme

Salt and black pepper, to taste

For Eggs
3 tablespoons distilled white vinegar

8 large eggs

*Instant polenta, an Italian cornmeal porridge, can be found in the Italian foods section of major grocery stores. Traditional (noninstant) polenta or coarse cornmeal can be used instead.

1. Line a 13-by-9-inch baking pan with parchment paper or plastic wrap; lightly coat with nonstick cooking spray. Prepare polenta according to package instructions; season to taste with salt and pepper. Spread warm polenta into prepared baking pan. Lay a sheet of plastic wrap on top, smoothing out the surface. Refrigerate for about 30 minutes, or until firm.

2. To prepare balsamic reduction, combine vinegar and brown sugar in a small saucepan over medium heat. Simmer for 10 to 15 minutes, or until thick, syrupy, and reduced by at least half. Transfer to a small dish to cool.

3. Preheat oven to 200ºF and place a baking sheet in oven. Heat 1 tablespoon of the olive oil in a large nonstick skillet over medium-high heat.

4. Using a 3-inch round cookie cutter, cut circles of the firm polenta and add to skillet, taking care not to crowd the pan. Cook for 2 to 3 minutes per side, or until lightly browned and crispy. Transfer to oven to keep warm and repeat with remaining rounds, adding the remaining 1 tablespoon olive oil as needed.

5. To prepare topping, melt butter in a large skillet over medium heat. When butter is melted and the foam has subsided, add shallots and cook for 2 minutes. Add mushrooms and cook, stirring occasionally, for 10 to 15 minutes, or until mushrooms begin to brown. Stir in herbs and salt and pepper to taste, and cook for 2 minutes more.

6. For poached eggs (see poaching tips, page 16), crack 1 egg into a small ramekin. Fill a saucepan with water to a depth of 2 inches. Add white vinegar and bring to a bare simmer over medium heat. Add egg and cook for 4½ to 5 minutes, or until whites are cooked and yolk is just starting to harden around the edges. Lift egg out of pan with a slotted spoon. Repeat with remaining eggs. (If eggs have cooled by the time you are ready to serve them, they can be reheated in simmering water for 20 to 30 seconds.)

7. Top each polenta cake with a poached egg and a spoonful of mushroom mixture; drizzle with balsamic reduction and serve.

CORNMEAL PANCAKES WITH BEER-BRAISED SHORT RIBS

makes 4 servings (about 16 pancakes) ★ *active time: 1 hour 30 minutes* ★ *total time: 5 hours*

Although we call them pancakes, these savory cornmeal medallions are nothing like their sweet breakfast counterparts. The hearty spiced short rib topping puts maple syrup to shame.

For Short Ribs

1 tablespoon extra-virgin olive oil

1½ pounds (about 4) beef short ribs

1 large yellow onion, chopped

1 jalapeño, seeded and chopped

1 (14.9-ounce) can beer, preferably a stout such as Guinness

1 cup beef broth

2 tablespoons light brown sugar, packed

2 tablespoons tomato paste

1 tablespoon honey

½ teaspoon ground cinnamon

½ teaspoon ground cumin

½ teaspoon salt

Freshly ground black pepper, to taste

For Pancakes

⅔ cup all-purpose flour

⅔ cup cornmeal

½ tablespoon granulated sugar

1 teaspoon baking powder

½ teaspoon salt

1 egg, lightly beaten

¾ cup whole milk

1 cup fresh corn kernels (from about 2 ears)

Olive oil, for cooking

1 Granny Smith apple, diced

1. Preheat oven to 300°F. Heat oil in a large Dutch oven or heavy bottomed, ovenproof saucepan over medium-high heat. Add ribs and sear for 5 to 7 minutes, turning every 45 seconds or so, until evenly browned on all sides. Transfer to a plate.

2. Reduce heat to medium and add onions and jalapeños to saucepan; cook for about 5 minutes, or until softened. Add beer and broth and cook for 1 minute, scraping any brown bits off the bottom of the pan. Stir in brown sugar, tomato paste, honey, cinnamon, cumin, salt, and pepper. Return ribs to pan and bring mixture to a simmer; cover, place pan in the oven, and bake for 2½ hours, turning ribs once halfway through cooking time, until meat is tender and shrinking off the bone.

3. Transfer ribs to a plate until cool enough to handle, then shred meat, discarding bones. Transfer liquid from the pan to a wide, shallow bowl. Place bowl in an ice bath or the refrigerator until completely cool and fat solidifies on top (this can be done up to 1 day ahead of time). Skim off and discard as much fat as possible.

4. Return liquid to saucepan; simmer over medium heat until thickened and reduced by about one-third, 15 to 18 minutes. Add shredded meat and stir until evenly coated with sauce and heated through.

5. To prepare pancakes, preheat oven to 200°F; place a baking sheet in oven. Whisk together flour, cornmeal, sugar, baking powder, and salt in a large bowl. Stir in egg and milk until dry ingredients are evenly moistened. Fold in corn kernels.

6. Heat a splash of olive oil in a large, nonstick skillet over medium-high heat. Drop batter by the tablespoonful into skillet, spreading it into 3-inch rounds. Cook for 1 to 2 minutes per side, or until golden brown. Transfer to oven to keep warm and repeat with remaining batter. To serve, top each pancake with a spoonful of short rib mixture and a bit of apple.

citrusy and sophisticated

GRAPEFRUIT RISOTTO WITH SEARED SCALLOPS

makes 2 servings ★ total time: 50 minutes

Notes of citrus and thyme make this date-night favorite truly delectable.
Topped with succulent seared scallops, this risotto is dressed to impress.

For Risotto

3 tablespoons unsalted butter, divided

1 large shallot, minced (about 1/3 cup)

1 cup arborio rice*

1/4 cup white wine

1 cup freshly squeezed grapefruit juice
(from 1 large grapefruit)

1 teaspoon fresh thyme, minced

Salt and black pepper, to taste

1/2 grapefruit, peeled and segmented

For Scallops

4 large scallops (about 1/2 pound)

Pinch salt and pepper

1 tablespoon unsalted butter

*Arborio rice is an Italian short-grain rice that becomes beautifully creamy when cooked, making it perfect for risotto. Look for it in the rice and grains or Italian foods aisle of your grocery store.

1. Bring 4 cups water to a simmer. Reduce heat; cover to keep warm.

2. In a large skillet, melt 2 tablespoons of the butter over medium-high heat. Stir in shallots and cook until translucent, about 2 minutes. Add rice and stir until fragrant and coated with fat, about 2 minutes more. Add wine and stir until completely absorbed.

3. Add grapefruit juice and simmer until fully absorbed, stirring constantly. Add warm water, 1/2 cup at a time, and stir constantly; wait until water is fully absorbed before adding the next 1/2 cup. Continue adding water and stirring until rice is tender and creamy, about 25 minutes. You may not need all the water; 3 cups or so may be sufficient. Stir in thyme, the remaining 1 tablespoon butter, and salt and pepper to taste, followed by grapefruit segments. Transfer to serving bowls.

4. Pat scallops completely dry; season with salt and pepper. Heat butter in a large nonstick skillet over medium-high heat until it is melted and the foam subsides. Add scallops and sear for 1 to 1 1/2 minutes per side, or until golden brown. Arrange scallops on top of risotto and serve.

true love

PIZZA OVER EASY

makes two 10-inch pizzas (about 4 servings) ★ active time: 30 minutes ★ total time: 45 minutes

We've long agreed that the key to a lasting relationship is pizza. And this one satisfies both of our pizza cravings: spicy arugula–pistachio pesto for Lindsay, a runny egg for Taylor, and delightfully melty cheese for us both.

For Pesto

4 cups packed (4 ounces) baby arugula, plus more for topping

2/3 cup extra-virgin olive oil

1/2 cup shelled pistachios

2 garlic cloves, roughly chopped

1/2 teaspoon red pepper flakes, or to taste

Salt and black pepper, to taste

For Crust

2 (9- to -10-ounce) balls pizza dough, store-bought or homemade (see page 60)

Cornmeal or semolina flour,* for dusting

For Topping

8 ounces mozzarella cheese, grated or thinly sliced (about 1 cup)

1/2 cup (2 ounces) shredded Parmesan cheese

2 large eggs

*Semolina is a coarse flour made from yellow durum wheat. Like cornmeal, it keeps the pizza from sticking to the cooking surface.

1. At least 45 minutes before making the pizza, position a rack in the lower third of the oven and place a baking stone on rack. Preheat oven to 500°F, giving the stone ample time to thoroughly preheat. (Alternatively, you can use a baking sheet and preheat it for as long as it takes for the oven to come to temperature.)

2. To prepare pesto, place arugula, oil, pistachios, garlic, and red pepper flakes in the bowl of a food processor or blender. Pulse until smooth, about 30 seconds. Season to taste with salt and pepper.

3. On a lightly floured work surface, roll or stretch dough into disks about 10 inches in diameter. Generously dust a pizza peel or the underside of a sheet pan with cornmeal or semolina flour. Lay 1 round of dough on the peel.

4. Spread half of pesto over dough. Sprinkle half of the cheeses on top. Crack 1 egg in the center of the dough.

5. Gently slide pizza onto the hot stone or baking pan. Bake until cheese is melted and egg white is cooked through, about 8 to 10 minutes; the edges of the crust should be golden brown. Remove from oven and let cool slightly prior to slicing. Top with fresh arugula. Repeat for second pizza.

★ ★ ★

Breakfast Pizza

Try topping with sausage, bacon, and other breakfast favorites to suit your taste.

Our favorite homemade pizza crust is made with a Neapolitan-style dough, producing a thin and crispy crust. The thyme and fennel seed give it an extra something special. *Makes 18 ounces (enough for two 10-inch pizzas). Total time: 10 hours.*

---

2 ¼ cups bread flour

¾ teaspoon salt

1 teaspoon whole fennel seeds

½ teaspoon dried thyme

½ teaspoon instant yeast

2 tablespoons extra-virgin olive oil

¾ cup plus 2 tablespoons
(7 ounces) cold water

All-purpose flour, for dusting

1. Whisk together flour, salt, fennel, thyme, and yeast in a large mixing bowl or the bowl of a stand mixer. With an electric mixer on low speed, mix in oil and cold water until no dry flour remains. Switch to the dough hook and mix on medium speed (or knead by hand) for 5 to 7 minutes, or until dough is smooth and slightly sticky. Add more flour as needed; the dough should come away from the sides of the bowl but still stick to the bottom.

2. Transfer dough to a lightly floured work surface. Lightly oil a baking dish or platter. Cut dough in half, and gently shape each piece into a ball. Place balls on prepared dish, cover with plastic wrap, and refrigerate overnight.

3. Remove dough from refrigerator and let rise at room temperature for 2 hours before baking. (See page 58 for baking instructions.)

Dough balls can be frozen instead of refrigerated: simply wrap each ball in plastic wrap and place inside a zippered freezer bag. Transfer to the refrigerator to thaw the day before you plan on baking.

for delicious make-ahead meals

HOW TO FREEZE HOMEMADE PIZZA

Frozen pizza is a convenience-food staple, but did you know you can make it yourself?

1. Prepare 1 batch of Pizza Dough (see page 60), divide it in thirds, and roll out each third into an 8-inch round. (These smaller pizzas fit perfectly inside a one-gallon zip-top freezer bag.) Bake at 500ºF on a thoroughly preheated pizza stone or baking sheet for 3 to 4 minutes, or until puffed.

2. Let crusts cool completely before adding toppings. Place pizzas on baking sheets dusted with cornmeal or semolina flour. Freeze for at least 3 to 4 hours, or until firm.

3. Wrap frozen pizzas tightly in a double layer of plastic wrap and place inside a freezer bag. Freeze for up to 2 months. When you're ready to bake, unwrap frozen pizzas and transfer to a baking pan or a thoroughly preheated pizza stone. Bake at 425ºF for 10 to 12 minutes, or until edges are golden brown and crispy.

the ultimate breakfast in a bun

SUNNY-SIDE-UP BURGERS

makes 4 burgers ★ total time: 40 minutes

"Put an egg on it" may very well become your mantra after you try this juicy burger, piled high with brunch-inspired toppings like sweet apricot preserves and crispy shoestring potatoes.

For Crispy Potatoes

2 tablespoons canola oil, plus more as needed

1 medium russet potato, peeled and cut into shoestrings or finely grated (see below)

For Burgers

1 pound ground sirloin

1 teaspoon Worcestershire sauce

1/4 teaspoon salt

1/4 teaspoon ground black pepper

4 burger buns, split and lightly toasted

For Toppings

4 medium or large eggs

1/4 cup apricot jam

4 slices pecorino cheese (optional)

4 leaves green leaf lettuce

1. To prepare potatoes, heat oil in a large skillet over medium-high heat. Drop potatoes by the rounded tablespoonful into skillet, and spread into a thin layer. Cook for 3 to 4 minutes, then flip and cook for 3 to 4 minutes more, or until both sides are golden brown and crispy. Transfer to a paper-towel-lined plate to drain.

2. To prepare burgers, use your hands or a spoon to combine beef with Worcestershire sauce, salt, and pepper. Divide into quarters; shape into four 1/2-inch-thick patties.

3. Return skillet to medium-high heat; add more oil if pan looks dry. Cook patties for about 3 minutes per side, or to desired doneness.

4. Heat a large nonstick skillet over medium heat. Coat lightly with oil or cooking spray. Add eggs, spacing them in skillet so they don't run together. Cook for 2 to 3 minutes, then carefully flip and cook for 30 seconds more. The yolk will be slightly runny; if you prefer a firmer egg, cook for an additional minute.

5. Spread a thin layer of jam inside buns. Arrange burger patties on bottom buns and top with cheese (if desired), crispy potatoes, fried egg, and lettuce. Top buns and serve.

★ ★ ★

Easy Shoestring Potatoes

There are gadgets that cut perfectly stringy shoestring potatoes, but you can easily cut them yourself if you've got a steady hand. A julienne peeler or citrus zester (*not* a Microplane) works well too. You can also simply grate the potatoes using a cheese grater.

Southern breakfast fusion

CHICKEN & BISCUIT WAFFLES

makes 4 servings ★ total time: 45 minutes

Chicken and waffles. Chicken and biscuits. Both are classic (albeit offbeat) Southern dishes. Fuse the two and you get savory fried chicken and biscoffles, or chicken and wiscuits, if you prefer. We love to serve this indulgent combo topped with a bright arugula salad.

For Chicken

2 large chicken breasts (about 2 pounds)

Salt and black pepper, to taste

Vegetable oil, for frying

²/₃ cup buttermilk

¹/₂ cup all-purpose flour

For Biscuit Waffles

1¹/₂ cups self-rising flour*

¹/₄ teaspoon salt

¹/₂ teaspoon freshly ground black pepper

¹/₄ cup (¹/₂ stick) cold unsalted butter, cut into pieces

1 cup buttermilk

Freshly tossed arugula salad for topping

*Self-rising flour is all-purpose flour premixed with salt and a leavener. If you don't have any, add 1¹/₂ teaspoons of baking powder and an additional 1¹/₄ teaspoons salt to 1¹/₂ cups all-purpose flour.

1. Place each chicken breast between 2 pieces of plastic wrap; pound to an even ¹/₂-inch thickness, then cut in half crosswise. Season generously with salt and pepper.

2. Fill a heavy skillet with oil to a depth of ¹/₄ inch. Bring to 350°F over medium heat. Place buttermilk in a wide, shallow bowl and all-purpose flour in another wide, shallow bowl.

3. Dredge chicken in buttermilk, followed by flour, shaking off excess. Add chicken to hot oil, 2 pieces at a time, and fry for 4 to 5 minutes per side, or until golden brown and cooked through.

4. For waffles, whisk together self-rising flour, salt, and pepper in a bowl. With a pastry blender or fork, cut butter into dry ingredients until mixture resembles coarse crumbs. Add buttermilk and stir with a fork until no dry flour remains.

5. Preheat a Belgian waffle iron according to the manufacturer's instructions. Scoop batter into waffle iron and cook until outside is golden brown and toasted. Repeat with remaining batter. Divide waffles among plates. Top each waffle with a piece of fried chicken and arugula salad and serve.

★ ★ ★

Arugula Salad with Lemon-Honey Dressing

★ 1 tablespoon olive oil ★ ¹/₂ tablespoon lemon juice (from ¹/₂ large lemon) ★ ¹/₂ tablespoon honey ★ Salt and pepper, to taste ★ 4 cups (4 ounces) arugula

Whisk together olive oil, lemon juice, and honey in a small bowl. Season to taste with salt and pepper. Drizzle over arugula and toss to coat.

smothered in sage cream sauce

━━✠ BREAKFAST SAUSAGE RAVIOLI ✠━━

makes about 30 ravioli (4 servings) ★ *active time: 50 minutes* ★ *total time: 1 hour*

Homemade ravioli is a special treat and well worth the extra time and effort. Filled with breakfast-spiced pork sausage, bacon, fluffy potato, and creamy ricotta, these surprisingly light ravioli are topped with a white wine and sage cream sauce.

For Filling

1 medium Yukon gold potato (about 5 ounces), roughly chopped

1/4 cup whole-milk ricotta cheese

1 strip bacon, finely diced

1/2 pound ground pork

1 teaspoon light brown sugar

1/2 teaspoon dried thyme

1/2 teaspoon garlic powder

1/4 teaspoon dried ground sage

1/4 teaspoon salt

1/4 teaspoon freshly ground black pepper

3/4 pound fresh pasta dough (see page 68)

For Sauce

1/2 cup white wine

1/4 cup heavy cream

1/4 cup (1/2 stick) unsalted butter

2 fresh sage leaves, chopped

Salt and pepper, to taste

Shaved or shredded Parmesan cheese, for topping

1. Bring a pot of salted water to a rolling boil. Add potatoes and cook for 5 to 7 minutes, or until tender. Transfer to a large bowl with a slotted spoon; smash with a fork or potato masher. Stir in ricotta cheese.

2. Cook bacon in a skillet over medium heat until it starts to brown, about 2 to 3 minutes. Add pork and cook for 2 minutes, breaking up any large pieces. Stir in brown sugar, spices, salt, and pepper and cook for about 6 minutes more, or until pork begins to brown. Transfer pork to bowl with potato mixture and stir to incorporate; taste and add additional salt and pepper, if desired. Set skillet aside; you will use the drippings to make the sauce.

3. For ravioli (see assembly tips, page 69), divide pasta dough into quarters and roll out into thin sheets. Lay 1 sheet on a lightly floured surface. Place teaspoons of filling an inch apart over entire sheet. With a pastry brush or your fingertip, brush water in the spaces between filling. Lay a second sheet of dough over the first and press around filling to seal. Cut into squares with a pastry wheel.

4. Bring a large pot of salted water to a rolling boil. Working in batches, boil ravioli for 7 to 8 minutes, or until tender. Transfer with a slotted spoon to serving dishes, reserving 1/4 cup pasta water.

5. To prepare sauce, return skillet with pork drippings to medium heat. Add wine and simmer for 2 minutes, scraping brown bits off the bottom of the pan. Add cream, butter, and sage and simmer until thickened slightly, 3 to 5 minutes, whisking constantly to prevent scorching. If needed, add reserved pasta water, a teaspoon at a time, until sauce is the consistency of thick cream. Spoon over ravioli and top with Parmesan cheese.

HOMEMADE PASTA DOUGH

Fresh homemade pasta is tender and flavorful, and well worth the time and effort it takes to make from scratch. Use this basic recipe for delicious homemade ravioli, or roll and slice for linguine, tagliatelle, or (our personal favorite) pappardelle—the only difference in the three being the thickness of the noodles. *Makes ³/₄ pound. Active time: 15 minutes. Total time: 45 minutes.*

1³/₄ cup "00" flour* or all-purpose flour

2 large eggs

¼ teaspoon salt

*00 flour is an extrafine Italian flour that makes for smooth and tender pasta. Find it at specialty grocers or online.

By Hand:

On a flat surface, sift the flour into a large pile; make a well in the center roughly the size of your fist. Add eggs to well along with ½ tablespoon of water and salt. With a fork, whisk the eggs, gradually incorporating the flour. Add more flour or water as needed, a teaspoon at a time, to form a firm dough. Knead dough for 2 to 3 minutes, or until smooth.

By Machine:

Combine flour and salt in the bowl of a stand mixer or a food processor. Add eggs and mix on medium speed or pulse until dough comes together in a ball. Switch to the dough hook/attachment and knead for 1 to 2 minutes, adding more water or flour as needed, a teaspoon at a time, to form a firm dough. Transfer to a lightly floured surface and knead by hand for 1 to 2 minutes, or until smooth. Wrap dough tightly in plastic wrap and let rest for 30 minutes before rolling out by hand or with a pasta roller and cutting into desired shape.

HOW TO MAKE RAVIOLI

Homemade ravioli can be made ahead and refrigerated or frozen until ready to use. Arrange in a single layer on baking sheets sprinkled with cornmeal or semolina flour; cover and refrigerate up to 1 day. You can also freeze them in zip-top bags for up to 1 month.

1. Divide rested pasta dough into quarters and run each quarter through a pasta roller to form a 12-by-4-inch rectangle. Lay 1 sheet on a lightly floured surface and place teaspoons of filling an inch apart over the entire sheet, remembering to leave space between filling and the edges of the sheet. A small cookie scoop can be helpful for dropping evenly sized dollops.

2. Lightly brush spaces around filling with water and then lay a second sheet of dough over the first. Press around the filling to seal.

3. Cut into squares with a pastry wheel (a tool that cuts and seals at the same time); if you don't have one, cut into squares using a knife and then crimp edges with a fork to seal.

SIDES & STARTERS

Perfect Hard-Boiled Eggs

whet your appetite

NOVA LOX BRUSCHETTA

makes 36 appetizer-size pieces ★ total time: 20 minutes

This simple toasted-bread appetizer comes together quickly yet looks impressive as part of a brunch spread. Nova lox pairs beautifully with tangy goat cheese and salty capers, and a sprinkling of caraway gives a flavor evocative of freshly baked rye bread.

1 large whole wheat baguette, sliced into 36 $\frac{3}{8}$-inch-thick slices

$\frac{3}{4}$ cup (6 ounces) soft goat cheese

1 tablespoon whole caraway seeds*

1 English (seedless) cucumber, thinly sliced

4 ounces Nova lox

$\frac{1}{4}$ small red onion, very thinly sliced

$\frac{1}{4}$ cup capers, drained and rinsed

*Caraway seeds are what give rye bread its distinctive flavor; you can find them in the spice aisle of any major grocery store. If you cannot find them, just omit them; there's no real substitute in terms of flavor.

1. Preheat broiler to high. Arrange bread slices on a baking sheet. Broil for 1 to 2 minutes, or until lightly golden and toasted.

2. Spread 1 teaspoon of goat cheese on each slice of bread; sprinkle with caraway seeds. Top each toast with a few cucumber slices and a piece of salmon. Finish with a pinch of red onion and a sprinkle of capers.

Lox, Nova Lox, Smoked Salmon, Gravlax

All three are types of cured salmon, so what's the difference? Lox is cured in a salt brine, whereas gravlax is cured in a dry mixture of salt, sugar, herbs, and spices. Lox that's described as Nova-style or Nova Scotia–style has also been cold-smoked, and its flavor typically is milder than that of lox. Although this recipe would work fine with any of the three, we prefer the milder Nova lox.

the ultimate appetizer

⇒⊱ MAPLE-GLAZED PORK MEATBALLS ⊰⇐

makes 24 meatballs ★ active time: 45 minutes ★ total time: 1 hour 30 minutes

The best part of breakfast is the moment when the maple syrup begins to seep into the sausage on the other side of your plate. Clearly pork and maple syrup were meant to be, so we put them together in what may be the perfect meatball.

For Meatballs

2 tablespoons extra-virgin olive oil

1 medium yellow onion, diced

1 small Granny Smith apple, peeled, cored, and finely diced (about 1 cup diced)

1 tablespoon grated or finely minced ginger (from a 1-inch piece)

2 garlic cloves, minced

1 pound ground pork

1 large egg

1/2 cup unseasoned breadcrumbs

1/4 cup milk

2 tablespoons pure maple syrup

1 teaspoon ground fennel seeds

1/2 teaspoon crushed red pepper flakes

1/2 teaspoon kosher salt

1/4 teaspoon ground black pepper

For Glaze

2 tablespoons pure maple syrup

2 teaspoons tomato paste

1/2 cup apple juice

2 teaspoons cider vinegar

1. Heat olive oil in a large skillet over medium heat. Add onions and cook until translucent, 7 to 10 minutes. Stir in apples, ginger, and garlic and cook for 1 to 2 minutes more. Remove from heat and let cool to lukewarm.

2. In a large bowl, combine pork, egg, breadcrumbs, milk, maple syrup, fennel, red pepper flakes, salt, and black pepper. Add lukewarm onion mixture and stir or mix with your hands until uniform. Roll by the tablespoon into 1-inch balls and arrange on a foil-lined baking sheet. Refrigerate for at least 30 minutes, or until set.

3. Preheat oven to 400°F. To prepare glaze, whisk together maple syrup, tomato paste, apple juice, and vinegar in a small saucepan. Bring to a simmer and cook over medium heat, stirring occasionally, until reduced by half, about 5 to 7 minutes. Transfer to a heat-proof bowl and let cool slightly.

4. Brush meatballs with half of the glaze and bake for 10 minutes. Remove from oven and brush with the remaining glaze. Bake for an additional 5 to 7 minutes, or until the internal temperature reaches 160°F. Serve warm.

not your grandmother's potato pancakes

ROOT VEGETABLE LATKES

makes about 20 pancakes ★ total time: 1 hour

We love latkes—the fried potato pancakes reminiscent of hash browns that are traditionally served at Hanukkah—and we especially love the ones Lindsay's grandmother makes (which, and we may be biased, are the best latkes ever). But we like to think that this version, made with a rainbow of potatoes, sweet potatoes, and beets, is a crispy and naturally sweet morsel even Grandma would enjoy.

2 large russet potatoes, peeled and grated (about 3 cups grated)*

1 large beet, peeled and grated (about 1½ cups grated)

1 large sweet potato, peeled and grated (about 1¼ cups grated)

½ large yellow onion, finely chopped (about ¼ cup chopped)

2 large eggs, lightly beaten

¼ cup all-purpose flour

¾ teaspoon salt

½ teaspoon ground black pepper

Canola oil, for frying

1 cup store-bought or homemade applesauce (page 78), for serving

1 cup sour cream (optional), for serving

*While you prep the other ingredients, soak potatoes in a bowl of cold water to keep them from turning brown.

1. Drain potatoes well. Place in a clean dishtowel or paper towels and squeeze to remove as much liquid as possible. Then spin them in a salad spinner lined with paper towels to force out even more liquid. (You want them as dry as possible, so the latkes hold together during frying.) Repeat with beets, sweet potatoes, and onions.

2. Preheat oven to 200°F. Line a baking sheet with two layers of paper towels and place in the oven. In a large bowl, thoroughly combine grated vegetables, onions, eggs, flour, salt, and pepper.

3. In a large nonstick skillet over medium heat, pour about ¼ cup of oil, or enough to cover the bottom of the skillet with a thin layer. When oil is hot but not smoking, spoon ¼ cup of potato mixture into pan, spreading out to a thin round with a fork or spatula. Working in batches so as not to overcrowd the skillet, cook latkes for 4 minutes per side, or until golden brown. Transfer cooked latkes to prepared baking sheet in oven to keep warm. Repeat with remaining potato mixture, adding more oil to skillet as necessary. Serve warm with applesauce and sour cream, if desired.

Leftover latkes can be wrapped and refrigerated or frozen; reheat on a baking sheet in a 350°F oven until crisp and heated through.

HOMEMADE APPLESAUCE

This fresh applesauce is delicious when made with a mix of sweet apple varieties, such as Gala, Golden Delicious, or Pink Lady. *Makes 1 cup. Total time: 30 minutes.*

4 large apples, peeled, cored, and coarsely chopped

1 teaspoon lemon juice

$\frac{1}{4}$ cup light brown sugar, packed

$\frac{1}{8}$ teaspoon ground cinnamon

1. In a medium saucepan bring apples, lemon juice, and $\frac{1}{3}$ cup water to a boil over medium heat, stirring occasionally. Simmer for 10 to 12 minutes, or until apples begin to break down. Add brown sugar and cinnamon and boil for 2 minutes more. Remove from heat.

2. For a chunky applesauce, mash mixture with a potato masher. For a smoother sauce, run through a food mill or pulse briefly in a food processor (but do not liquefy). Refrigerated in an airtight container, applesauce will keep for up to 1 week.

TOMATO PEACH JAM

This spicy, sweet, and savory jam is a scrumptious companion for beignets (page 81), burgers, and bruschetta. We also love it spread inside a grilled cheese sandwich—like having your grilled cheese and tomato soup all in one! *Makes 2 cups. Total time: 45 minutes.*

2 pounds roma or plum tomatoes (about 8 tomatoes)

1 large peach

1 hot red pepper (such as jalapeño or Thai chile), finely minced

½ cup granulated sugar

1 tablespoon lemon juice

1. Bring a large pot of water to a gentle boil. Cut an x-shaped slit in the bottom of each tomato. Boil tomatoes for 30 seconds. Remove with a slotted spoon and place immediately in a bowl of ice water to stop cooking. When cool to touch, the skins will peel off easily. Peel and coarsely chop tomatoes, reserving juices. You should end up with about 3 cups of chopped tomato. Do the same thing to peel peach; remove pit and chop.

2. In a saucepan, stir together tomatoes, peaches, peppers, sugar, and lemon juice. Bring to a boil over medium heat. Cook until thickened and reduced by one-third, about 30 minutes, stirring regularly. If you want a smoother consistency, let jam cool slightly, then process in a blender or food processor until smooth. Refrigerated in an airtight container, jam will keep for up to 1 week.

think outside the doughnut

PARMESAN BEIGNETS

makes 36 beignets ★ *active time: 1 hour* ★ *total time: 4 hours*

Beignets (pronounced *ben-YAYS*) are French pastries made from deep-fried dough and frequently topped with a mountain of confectioners' sugar. They're often called the precursor to the modern American doughnut. We make ours with a Parmesan dough and serve them with a spicy tomato-peach jam that's both sweet and savory.

¾ cup whole milk, lukewarm

1¼ teaspoons (½ package) instant yeast

2 cups bread flour*

1 large egg, room temperature

1 cup grated Parmesan cheese, divided

2 tablespoons unsalted butter, softened

1 tablespoon granulated sugar

¼ teaspoon salt

¼ teaspoon freshly ground black pepper

Vegetable or peanut oil, for frying

1 cup tomato jam, store-bought or homemade (page 79)

*Bread flour is a high-protein flour specially formulated for bread baking. The extra protein aids in the formation of gluten. All-purpose flour can be used in a pinch, although the dough won't be quite as elastic.

1. Pour milk into the bowl of a stand mixer. Sprinkle yeast on top; let sit for 5 minutes, or until frothy. Add flour, egg, ⅓ cup of the Parmesan, butter, sugar, salt, and pepper, and mix with the paddle attachment until dough comes together. Switch to the dough hook (or turn dough out onto a floured surface) and knead for 5 to 7 minutes, or until dough is smooth and elastic. Place in an oiled bowl; cover and let rise in a warm place for 1 to 2 hours, or until doubled in volume.

2. Turn out dough onto a floured surface. Roll into a ½-inch-thick sheet. Using a circle cutter, cut into 1½-inch rounds and arrange on a lightly floured or parchment-lined baking sheet with 1 inch between rounds. Cover loosely with plastic wrap and let stand for 15 to 20 minutes, or until doubled in size.

3. Fill a heavy saucepan with oil to a depth of at least 2 inches; bring to 350°F over medium heat. Line a large platter or baking sheet with paper towels.

4. Gently drop dough rounds into the hot oil, a few at a time, taking care not to overcrowd pan. Fry until golden brown, about 30 seconds per side. Transfer to prepared baking sheet to drain. Repeat with remaining rounds, monitoring oil temperature as you go and, if necessary, waiting for temperature to return to 350°F before frying more dough.

5. As soon as beignets are cool enough to handle, toss with the remaining ⅔ cup Parmesan cheese to coat. Serve warm with tomato jam for dipping.

spicy cheesy goodness

══ ◄ HABANERO-CHEDDAR BREAD PUDDING ► ══

makes 6 to 8 side servings ★ active time: 30 minutes ★ total time: 1 hour 40 minutes

Bread pudding is no longer just for dessert. This savory rendition is delicious alone or served as a side dish with your preferred protein. Cheesy and creamy, with a hit of heat from the habaneros, it combines convenience and comfort all in one pan.

1 (10- to 12-ounce) loaf day-old French bread, cut into ¾-inch cubes (about 9 cups)

1 poblano pepper, cored, seeded, and quartered

1 tablespoon extra-virgin olive oil

1 large yellow onion, chopped

4 garlic cloves, minced

4 slices prosciutto, chopped into ¼-inch pieces

1 habanero pepper, cored, seeded, and minced

2 cups shredded cheddar cheese, (6 ounces), divided

5 large eggs

2½ cups whole milk

½ teaspoon salt

½ teaspoon dried oregano

1. Preheat broiler to high. Spread bread cubes in a single layer on 2 rimmed baking sheets. Broil, 1 sheet at a time, until bread is toasted and lightly golden brown, about 1 to 2 minutes. Repeat with second sheet. Transfer toasted cubes to a 13-by-9-inch baking pan.

2. Arrange poblanos on a baking sheet, skin side up. Broil until skin starts to blister and darken. Transfer to a cutting board until cool enough to handle, and then roughly chop.

3. Turn oven temperature to 350°F. Heat olive oil in a large skillet over medium-high heat. Cook onion until translucent, 3 to 5 minutes. Add garlic and cook for 1 minute more. Add prosciutto and habaneros and cook until starting to brown, about 4 minutes. Finally, add roasted poblanos and toss to incorporate. Remove from heat and let cool to lukewarm.

4. Sprinkle onion mixture evenly over bread cubes, followed by 1½ cups of the cheese. Whisk together eggs, milk, salt, and oregano and pour over bread mixture. Toss to combine. Sprinkle remaining ½ cup cheese on top.

5. Bake for about 45 to 55 minutes, or until top of pudding is puffed and golden brown and center is set. Remove pan from oven and let cool for 10 to 15 minutes before serving.

the best of breakfast in a jar

BACON JAM

makes about 2 cups ★ *total time: 3 hours*

A magical cross between ketchup and fruit preserves—but with bacon—this jam just might be the king of all condiments. The rich flavor of bacon is complemented by hints of coffee, citrus, maple syrup, and bourbon.

1 pound sliced bacon, cut crosswise into 1/2-inch pieces

1 large yellow onion, chopped

2 garlic cloves, minced

1 cup brewed coffee

1/2 cup cider vinegar

1/2 cup orange juice

1/4 cup pure maple syrup

2 tablespoons light brown sugar, packed

1 teaspoon orange zest

1/4 teaspoon ground ginger

1/8 teaspoon freshly ground black pepper, or to taste

1/4 cup bourbon

1. Heat a large heavy skillet or Dutch oven over medium-high heat. Cook bacon until it starts to brown, 10 to 12 minutes. With a slotted spoon, transfer bacon to a paper-towel-lined plate. Drain off all but 2 tablespoons of the bacon fat in skillet.

2. Reduce heat to medium. Add onions and garlic and cook until onion begins to soften, about 5 minutes, stirring frequently so garlic does not burn. Return bacon to skillet and add coffee, vinegar, orange juice, maple syrup, brown sugar, orange zest, ginger, and pepper. Reduce heat to low and simmer for 45 minutes. Transfer mixture to a food processor and pulse briefly until finely chopped. Return mixture to pan and cook for another 15 minutes, stirring occasionally. Add bourbon and gently simmer for 30 minutes more, or until jam is thick, syrupy, and dark in color; if at any point the mixture starts to stick to the bottom of the pan and starts to look more like paste than jam, add water, 1/4 cup at a time. Remove from heat and let cool slightly. Refrigerated in an airtight container, bacon jam will keep for 3 to 4 weeks.

★ ★ ★

Goes with Everything

Our favorite way to eat bacon jam is spread on a grilled cheese sandwich, but it's also great as a condiment for burgers, dolloped on biscuits or blueberry pancakes, or paired with a wonderfully stinky cheese on crackers.

easy, elegant anytime food

⚞ ASPARAGUS PASTRY TART ⚟

makes 4 servings ★ active time: 15 minutes ★ total time: 30 minutes

This tart brings the best of brunch to your dinner table. With lemon-herb ricotta, tender asparagus, and salty pancetta, it's a spring fling served in a puff pastry crust.

---

1 sheet frozen puff pastry, thawed according to package directions

1/2 cup whole-milk ricotta cheese

2 tablespoons finely chopped fresh chives

1/2 teaspoon finely chopped fresh thyme

1/2 teaspoon lemon zest (from 1/2 large lemon)

Salt and black pepper, to taste

1 bunch (1 pound) thin asparagus spears, trimmed

1 tablespoon extra-virgin olive oil

2 ounces pancetta,* cut into 1/4-inch cubes

1 ounce pecorino cheese,** grated

*Pancetta is an Italian cured pork belly product that's similar to bacon, although it is not smoked. For this recipe, buy it sliced thick or cubed if you can. Bacon would make a good substitute in a pinch.

**Pecorino is a hard Italian sheep's milk cheese with a distinct nutty flavor. Parmesan is a good substitute.

1. Preheat oven to 400°F. Place puff pastry on a baking sheet lined with parchment paper. Using a sharp knife, lightly score a border 1/2 inch inside the edge of the dough, taking care not to cut completely through. Bake until pastry is just starting to puff, about 10 minutes.

2. In a small bowl, mix ricotta, chives, thyme, and lemon zest with a spoon. Season with salt and pepper. Spread ricotta mixture onto pastry, spreading in an even layer inside the scored border. Lay asparagus in a single layer on top, alternating ends and tips (see photograph); brush with olive oil. Bake for about 15 minutes, or until asparagus is tender and pastry is golden brown.

3. While tart bakes, cook pancetta in a small skillet over medium heat until browned and crispy. Sprinkle over tart; top with cheese. Cut into slices and serve immediately.

savory spiced chicken, all rolled up

MOROCCAN CHICKEN CINNAMON ROLLS

makes 12 rolls (about 3 servings) ★ *active time: 1 hour* ★ *total time: 1 hour 30 minutes*

These savory "cinnamon rolls" were inspired by Moroccan *pastilla*, sweet and savory meat pies laced with cinnamon and wrapped in a phyllo-like dough. Our version is a spiral of spiced shredded chicken in a flaky puff pastry crust, perfect for the dinner table.

1 tablespoon extra-virgin olive oil

4 bone-in chicken thighs
(1½ pounds)

1 medium yellow onion, chopped

2 teaspoons ground cinnamon

¾ teaspoon ground cumin

½ teaspoon ground ginger

½ teaspoon ground turmeric

½ teaspoon freshly ground
black pepper

½ teaspoon ground coriander

¼ teaspoon salt

1 cup chicken broth

1 sheet frozen puff pastry,* thawed
according to package directions

¼ cup sliced almonds

*Puff pastry dough can be found in the freezer section of most major grocery stores; look for it near the pie crusts. Thaw it in the refrigerator overnight or at room temperature for about 30 minutes.

1. Heat oil in a large, heavy saucepan over medium-high heat. Add chicken and cook for 5 minutes per side, or until lightly browned. Transfer to a plate; pour off any excess fat from the pan. Add onions; reduce heat to medium and cook until softened and translucent, about 5 minutes. Add spices and stir to coat. Add chicken broth and stir, scraping up any brown bits from the bottom of the pan.

2. Return chicken to pan. Cover and simmer for 35 minutes, flipping once, until meat is tender and starts to come off the bone. Transfer chicken to a large bowl to cool slightly, and then shred meat, discarding skin and bones.

3. Return pan to medium-high heat and simmer liquid until thickened, about 16 to 18 minutes. Return shredded chicken to pan and toss to coat. Remove from heat and let cool slightly.

4. Preheat oven to 400°F. Line a baking sheet with aluminum foil; grease with cooking spray.

5. On a lightly floured surface, roll out puff pastry to a 9-by-12-inch rectangle. Spread chicken in a thin, even layer on top of pastry. Roll pastry fairly tightly up the long side to create a 12-inch log. Pinch along the edge to seal. With a sharp serrated knife, cut into twelve 1-inch slices. Arrange rolls on prepared baking sheet, leaving 1 inch between them. Sprinkle almonds over top. Bake for 20 to 22 minutes, or until pastry is puffed and lightly golden. Serve warm.

Chicken rolls are a great party appetizer. Make a meal by pairing them with a light salad and wild rice or couscous.

coffee-spiked and well-liked

⟝ ESPRESSO BAKED BEANS ⟞

makes 6 to 8 servings ★ *active time: 45 minutes* ★ *total time: 18 hours*

The long baking time gives these baked beans a rich, complex flavor with plenty of sweetness and subtle coffee undertones. They are a great side dish at a summer barbecue or alongside a comforting winter meal.

1 pound dried great northern beans*

8 slices (½ pound) bacon, cut into ½-inch pieces

1 large yellow onion, chopped

1 large carrot, chopped

2 jalapeños, seeded and chopped

2 cups vegetable broth, plus more as needed

1 cup brewed coffee

½ cup light brown sugar, packed

2 tablespoons unsulphured molasses

2 tablespoons tomato paste

2 tablespoons cider vinegar

2 teaspoons instant espresso** or coffee powder

Salt and black pepper, to taste

*This is a popular type of white bean that absorbs flavors very well, making it perfect for this dish. Look for dried great northern beans in the rice and beans aisle or in the bulk foods section

**Instant espresso powder can be found in the coffee aisle of most major grocery stores or online. You can substitute instant coffee powder, but the coffee flavor will not be as intense.

1. Soak beans for 8 to 10 hours or overnight in just enough water to completely cover them.

2. Preheat oven to 250°F. Position a rack in the bottom third of the oven.

3. Cook bacon in a Dutch oven or a heavy-bottomed, ovenproof pot over medium-high heat until fat is rendered and bacon is just starting to brown, about 10 minutes. With a slotted spoon, transfer bacon to a paper towel-lined plate. Pour off all but 2 tablespoons of the bacon fat in the pot.

4. Return pot to medium heat; add onions, carrots, and jalapeños and cook until softened, about 5 to 7 minutes. Return bacon to pot; stir in vegetable broth, coffee, brown sugar, molasses, tomato paste, vinegar, and espresso powder.

5. Drain beans, reserving soaking liquid. Add enough water to soaking liquid to equal 1 cup and add to pot. Add beans and stir.

6. Increase heat to medium-high and bring to a simmer; place pot in oven, cover, and bake for 3 hours.

7. Remove pot from oven and give beans a good stir; add additional vegetable broth, ¼ cup at a time, if beans look too dry. Stir and bake for another 1 to 3 hours, checking periodically and adding more vegetable broth as necessary, until beans are tender and liquid is thickened. Season with salt and pepper.

wedges of fluffy egg and cheese

SCRAMBLED EGG & SALMON QUESADILLAS

makes 2 quesadillas ★ total time: 40 minutes

Ultra-creamy scrambled eggs are studded with smoked salmon and leeks and sandwiched between two crispy tortillas to make a unique quesadilla that has no shortage of flavor.

1 leek, sliced into thin rings*
(about 2 cups sliced)

1 tablespoon vegetable oil,
plus more for brushing

2 tablespoons vegetable broth

4 large eggs

2 tablespoons crème fraîche
or sour cream

Pinch each salt and black pepper

2 ounces smoked salmon,
cut into bite-sized pieces, divided

4 10-inch flour tortillas

½ cup grated fontina
or Gruyère cheese, divided

*When preparing leeks, trim off the roots and very bottom of the bulb; use the white and light green parts only. Discard the darker green portion, which is too tough to eat.

1. Place leeks in a large bowl of cold water; slosh them around to separate rings and wash completely (any dirt stuck between the layers will fall to the bottom of the bowl). Remove with a slotted spoon and drain completely.

2. Heat oil in a 10-inch nonstick skillet over medium heat. Add leeks and cook until translucent and just starting to brown, about 5 to 7 minutes. Add vegetable broth and cook until no liquid remains, 2 to 3 minutes more. Transfer half of the leeks to a bowl.

3. In a bowl, whisk eggs with crème fraîche. Add salt and pepper. Pour half of egg mixture into skillet with leeks. Sprinkle with half of salmon. Cover and cook until top of mixture is beginning to set but still slightly underdone, 5 to 7 minutes. Top with 1 tortilla. Brush top of tortilla with a little oil, and carefully flip entire quesadilla with a large spatula. Sprinkle with half of cheese, then top with a second tortilla; brush with oil.

4. Cook until bottom tortilla begins to brown and blister, then flip and cook until both sides are evenly browned. Transfer to a cutting board and cut into wedges. Repeat for second quesadilla and serve.

★ ★ ★

Breakfast Quesadillas

★ **Scrambled Egg & Veggie Quesadillas:** Add pieces of zucchini, mushrooms, or artichoke hearts to the skillet when cooking the leeks.

★ **Steak & Cheese Quesadillas:** Replace salmon with bite-sized pieces of leftover steak and top with shredded cheddar or Monterey Jack cheese.

★ **Southwest Chicken Quesadillas:** Add pieces of shredded roasted chicken in place of salmon and top with spicy pepper jack cheese and salsa.

crunchy munchy chips for dipping

═══ GARLIC BAGEL CHIPS ═══

makes 8 servings (about 8 cups chips) ★ active time: 30 minutes ★ total time: 45 minutes

A great way to use up leftover bagels, these crispy chips are seasoned with garlic and herbs. They're delicious served with a flavorful cream cheese and artichoke dip.

4 everything bagels, sliced into ¼-inch-thick wedges

¼ cup extra-virgin olive oil

1 teaspoon garlic powder

1 teaspoon dried parsley

½ teaspoon salt

½ teaspoon freshly ground black pepper

1. Preheat oven to 350°F.

2. In a bowl, toss bagel slices with oil, garlic powder, parsley, salt, and pepper until evenly coated. Divide evenly between 2 baking sheets and arrange in a single layer. Bake for 18 to 20 minutes, rotating baking sheets from top to bottom once during cooking, until golden brown and crispy.

★ ★ ★

Cream Cheese & Artichoke Dip

★ 1 (14-ounce) can artichoke hearts in oil, drained and roughly chopped (about 2 cups) ★ 2 ounces sun-dried tomatoes packed in oil, chopped (about ¼ cup) ★ ¼ small onion, diced (about ¼ cup) ★ 2 garlic cloves, minced ★ Pinch salt, plus more to taste ★ Pinch freshly ground black pepper, plus more to taste ★ 8 ounces cream cheese, room temperature ★ ½ cup grated Parmesan cheese ★ ½ cup plain Greek yogurt

Heat a skillet over medium-high heat. Add artichoke hearts, sun-dried tomatoes, onion, and garlic and cook, stirring, until softened, 3 to 5 minutes. Season with a pinch each of salt and pepper. Transfer to a food processor and add cream cheese, Parmesan cheese, and yogurt; pulse until smooth. Season to taste with salt and pepper. Dip can be made a day ahead; store covered in the refrigerator and bring to room temperature before serving.

Makes about 3 cups.

fluffy, flaky, and oh so cute

MINI BLT BISCUITS

makes 12 mini sandwiches ★ active time: 20 minutes ★ total time: 30 minutes

The classic combination of salty bacon, crisp lettuce, and juicy tomato is even better on a biscuit. These tasty little bites are reminiscent of breakfast sandwiches, yet their miniature size makes them perfect party appetizers.

For Biscuits
2 cups self-rising flour*

1/4 teaspoon salt

1/4 teaspoon freshly ground black pepper

1/4 cup unsalted butter, cut into cubes

2/3 cup buttermilk

Self-rising or all-purpose flour, for dusting

For Honey Dijon Mustard
2 tablespoons Dijon mustard

2 tablespoons honey

Salt and freshly ground black pepper, to taste

For Sandwiches
6 pieces green-leaf lettuce, torn into 2 1/2-inch pieces

1 large or 2 medium avocados, pitted and sliced

3 medium (tennis-ball-size) tomatoes, sliced

8 slices cooked bacon, cut in thirds

*If you don't have self-rising flour, substitute 2 cups all-purpose flour, 2 teaspoons baking powder, and an additional 1/4 teaspoon salt.

1. Preheat oven to 400°F. Sift together self-rising flour, salt, and pepper into a large bowl. Using a fork or pastry blender, cut in butter until mixture resembles coarse crumbs. With a fork, stir in buttermilk until dough comes together.

2. Turn out dough onto a floured surface and dust dough with flour. Pat dough into a roughly 1-inch-thick rectangle and fold in half. Repeat this patting and folding step 3 or 4 more times; this will create flaky layers in the dough, but be careful not to overwork it or your biscuits will be tough.

3. Press dough into a 1/2-inch-thick rectangle and cut into rounds with a 2 1/4-inch circle cutter. Reroll scraps only once and cut into rounds (note: these second-roll biscuits will not rise as tall as the first biscuits you cut). Arrange rounds an inch apart on a baking sheet. Bake until tops are lightly golden brown, about 10 minutes.

4. For the honey mustard, whisk together mustard, honey, salt, and pepper.

5. When biscuits are cool enough to handle, split them in half using a fork to gently pry the layers apart. Spread honey mustard onto each biscuit bottom. Top with lettuce, avocado slices, tomato, and 2 pieces of bacon. Close sandwiches, secure with a toothpick, and serve.

the perfect bite-sized appetizer

MINI ZUCCHINI & PESTO QUICHES

makes 24 mini quiches ★ active time: 20 minutes ★ total time: 35 minutes

The problem with most quiches is the crust: it can be soggy and lackluster, and the crust-to-filling ratio is never enough. Shrinking these quiches, which are packed with garlicky zucchini and bright pesto, into mini pop-in-your-mouth proportions and baking them in crispy paper-thin phyllo shells solves both problems quite nicely.

24 store-bought or homemade phyllo cups (page 100)

1 garlic clove, minced

1 small zucchini, grated (about 1 cup grated)

3 large eggs

½ cup heavy cream

Pinch each salt and black pepper

For Pesto

1 cup packed fresh basil leaves

3 tablespoons grated Parmesan cheese

2 tablespoons heavy cream

1 tablespoon extra-virgin olive oil

1 garlic clove, roughly chopped

¼ teaspoon salt

Freshly ground black pepper, to taste

1. Preheat oven to 400°F. Place a phyllo cup in each well of a mini muffin tin.

2. Heat a skillet over medium heat. Lightly spray with cooking spray or brush with ½ teaspoon olive oil. Add garlic and cook for 1 minute; stir in zucchini and cook for 2 to 3 minutes more, until it is just tender and the pan is mostly dry. Drop a scant teaspoon of zucchini mixture into each phyllo cup.

3. Whisk together eggs, cream, salt, and pepper.

4. To prepare pesto, place basil, cheese, cream, oil, and garlic in the bowl of a food processor. Pulse until smooth; season with salt and pepper. Whisk pesto into egg mixture.

5. Spoon egg mixture into phyllo cups, about 1 tablespoon per cup or enough to just barely fill (store-bought cups are smaller and will require less filling than homemade). Bake for 13 to 15 minutes, or until tops are puffed and just starting to brown. Serve warm.

★ ★ ★

These mini quiches are an easy make-ahead meal. Prepare them as above, let them cool, and then freeze them in a zip-top freezer bag. Reheat in a 350°F oven for 10 to 12 minutes, or until heated through.

MINI PHYLLO CUPS

Don't be intimidated by what you've heard about phyllo: working with this dough, which is sold in delicate sheets, is easy. These cups can be used for mini quiches (like the ones on page 98) or mini spanakopita (a Greek spinach and feta dish) as well as for sweeter applications. Fill them with chocolate mousse, pastry cream, or a nut-and-honey mixture for a treat reminiscent of baklava. *Makes 24 cups. Total time: 35 minutes.*

15 sheets (½ package) phyllo dough

6 tablespoons unsalted butter, melted

1. Preheat oven to 375°F. Lightly spray a mini muffin tin with cooking spray.

2. Lay 1 sheet of phyllo dough on a flat surface. To prevent dough from drying out as you work, keep the remaining dough covered with plastic wrap, a clean, damp dish towel, or both. Brush sheet lightly with melted butter, then top with a second sheet of dough. Continue brushing and stacking until you have a stack of 5 sheets.

3. Cut out rounds using a 3¼-inch circle cutter; you should be able to get about 8 rounds. Gently place each round in a well of the mini muffin tin.

4. Repeat with remaining dough; you should end up with 24 cups total. Bake cups for 8 to 10 minutes, or until edges are lightly golden and bottoms are puffed. Cool completely before using.

★ ★ ★

When it comes to phyllo, work with one sheet at a time, keeping the rest of the sheets covered with plastic wrap or a damp cloth to prevent them from drying out and becoming unworkable.

ROSEMARY & OLIVE OIL SCONES

With a light and delicate texture, these savory scones are perfectly flavored with the delicate herbal note of rosemary. But feel free to experiment with other mix-ins, such as thyme, chives, or Parmesan cheese. *Makes 8 scones. Active time: 10 minutes. Total time: 30 minutes.*

2 cups all-purpose flour

1 tablespoon baking powder

½ teaspoon kosher salt

¼ teaspoon finely chopped fresh rosemary, or more to taste

6 tablespoons cold unsalted butter, cut into cubes

½ cup whole milk, plus more as needed

2 tablespoons olive oil, plus more for brushing

Coarse sea salt, to taste

1. Preheat oven to 375°F.

2. In a large bowl, whisk together flour, baking powder, kosher salt, and rosemary. Using a pastry blender or fork, cut butter into dry ingredients until mixture resembles coarse crumbs. Add milk and oil and stir with a fork until evenly moistened. If dough is crumbly, add more milk, 1 tablespoon at a time, until dough comes together.

3. Gather dough into a mass and turn it out onto a lightly floured surface, kneading as necessary to incorporate any crumbs but taking care not to overwork it. Press into a ½-inch-thick circle about 8 inches in diameter. Cut into 8 wedges. Arrange on baking sheet; brush lightly with oil and sprinkle with sea salt.

4. Bake for 18 to 20 minutes, or until bottoms are lightly golden. Let cool for 2 minutes before serving. Leftover scones can be refrigerated in an airtight container for up to 2 days; warm in a 350°F oven prior to serving.

★ ★ ★

★ **Herb & Cheese Scones:** Add ½ cup grated Parmesan cheese and substitute or supplement rosemary with chopped fresh herbs such as thyme and oregano.

classic with a kick

➤ BLOODY MARY TOMATO SOUP ➤

makes 4 servings ★ active time: 45 minutes ★ total time: 1 hour 30 minutes

Classic tomato soup gets a makeover with hints of celery, Worcestershire sauce, and spicy Tabasco for the essence of the famous brunch-time cocktail. Served warm or cold, it goes great with a grilled cheese or Rosemary & Olive Oil Scones (page 101).

3 tablespoons extra-virgin olive oil, divided

2 pounds ripe tomatoes (about 3 to 5 large), sliced 3/4 inch thick

Salt and freshly ground black pepper, to taste

1 large yellow onion, chopped

1 celery stalk, chopped

1 large carrot, peeled and chopped

2 cloves garlic, minced

1/2 cup dry white wine

1 cup vegetable broth

1 1/2 teaspoons Worcestershire sauce

1 teaspoon Tabasco sauce, or to taste

1 teaspoon granulated sugar

1/2 teaspoon celery salt

1. Preheat oven to 400ºF. Line a baking sheet with aluminum foil and brush foil with 1 tablespoon of the oil.

2. Arrange tomato slices in a single layer on sheet, drizzle with another 1 tablespoon of oil, and season with salt and pepper. Bake for 30 minutes, then broil on high for 4 minutes, or until tops are lightly browned.

3. In a large saucepan, heat the remaining 1 tablespoon oil over medium heat. Cook onions, celery, carrot, and garlic, stirring occasionally, for 9 to 10 minutes, or until softened. Add wine and cook for another 4 minutes, or until most of the liquid has evaporated. Stir in roasted tomatoes and any juices, 3/4 cup water, vegetable broth, Worcestershire sauce, Tabasco, sugar, celery salt, and pepper to taste. Simmer for 30 minutes, stirring occasionally. Let cool slightly.

4. Blend in a food processor or blender (in batches if necessary) until smooth. Return to saucepan and warm over low heat until heated through; taste and adjust seasoning if necessary.

mix up your salad routine

➤ STRAWBERRIES & GREENS ➤
WITH GINGER-SCALLION DRESSING

makes 4 side servings ★ *total time: 20 minutes*

Mix up your routine with this delightful combination. The hard-boiled egg makes it heartier than your average salad. No need for a sugary dressing here; the strawberries provide a natural sweetness that pairs perfectly with the savory eggs and crunchy croutons.

For Croutons

2 cups day-old bread cubes

1 tablespoon olive oil

¼ teaspoon freshly ground black pepper

⅛ teaspoon salt

For Dressing

3 green onions, trimmed and roughly chopped

¼ cup extra-virgin olive oil, plus more as needed

1½ teaspoons minced ginger (from a 1-inch piece)

1½ tablespoons freshly squeezed lime juice

2 teaspoons agave nectar or honey

Salt and black pepper, to taste

For Salad

1 (5-ounce) bag mixed baby greens or spinach

1 pint strawberries, sliced

4 hard-boiled eggs, quartered

1. Preheat oven to 400°F. Lightly oil a large baking sheet.

2. Place bread in a large bowl. Drizzle oil over bread, add salt and pepper, and toss to combine. Spread cubes in a single layer on prepared baking sheet. Bake for 8 to 10 minutes, or until golden brown. Set aside.

3. To prepare dressing, combine green onions, oil, ginger, lime juice, and agave nectar in a food processor or blender. Pulse until smooth. If necessary, add more oil, a tablespoon at a time, until dressing reaches desired consistency. Season with salt and pepper.

4. In a large bowl, toss greens with dressing. Divide among serving dishes. Top with strawberries, eggs, and croutons.

★ ★ ★

Perfect Hard-Boiled Eggs

Place eggs in a large pot covered by 1 to 2 inches of water. Bring to a boil over high heat, then immediately cover and remove from heat. Let stand for 16 minutes. Remove eggs with a slotted spoon and place them in a bowl filled with ice water to stop the cooking. Let eggs cool completely, then drain and peel. Eggs can be boiled ahead of time; refrigerate in an airtight container until ready to use.

DRINKS & DESSERTS

bacon: it's what's for dessert

⇉ MAPLE BACON CUPCAKES ⇇

makes 12 cupcakes ★ active time: 45 minutes ★ total time: 1 hour

Though the recent food trend of incorporating bacon into dessert can be overdone, we think that, when used strategically, this crisp and salty breakfast meat can enhance a sweet treat in miraculous ways. These maple-infused cupcakes feature a simple candied bacon topping, but that tiny addition makes all the difference.

For Cupcakes
1½ cups all-purpose flour

1 teaspoon baking powder

½ teaspoon baking soda

½ teaspoon salt

½ cup (1 stick) unsalted butter, room temperature

½ cup light brown sugar, packed

2 large eggs, room temperature

¼ cup pure maple syrup

½ teaspoon pure vanilla extract

⅓ cup buttermilk

For Chocolate Buttercream
¾ cup (1½ sticks) unsalted butter, room temperature

½ cup cocoa powder, sifted

2½ cups confectioners' sugar, sifted

2 tablespoons maple syrup

⅛ teaspoon maple extract* (optional)

2 tablespoons heavy cream, more or less as needed

For Topping
4 slices Candied Bacon (page 110)

*Find maple extract near the vanilla extract in your local grocery store.

1. Preheat oven to 350°F. Line a muffin pan with cupcake papers.

2. In a bowl, sift together flour, baking powder, baking soda, and salt. Set aside.

3. In a large mixing bowl or the bowl of a stand mixer, beat together butter and brown sugar with an electric mixer on medium speed until light and fluffy, 2 to 3 minutes. Add eggs, 1 at a time, mixing well after each addition. Mix in maple syrup and vanilla extract.

4. Mix in dry ingredients, a little at a time, until incorporated. Beat in buttermilk on low speed until just incorporated.

5. Fill cupcake liners with a scant ¼ cup of batter (cups should be just under two-thirds full). Bake for 18 to 20 minutes, or until a toothpick inserted in the center comes out clean. Transfer pan to a cooling rack; when pan is cool enough to handle, place cupcakes on rack to cool completely.

6. To prepare buttercream, beat butter with an electric mixer on medium-high speed for 1 to 2 minutes, or until fluffy. Add cocoa powder and beat until smooth. Slowly beat in confectioners' sugar, ½ cup at a time, until mixture is smooth. Beat in maple syrup and maple extract (if using). Add cream as needed and beat on medium-high speed until light and fluffy, 2 to 3 minutes.

7. Generously spread or pipe frosting onto cooled cupcakes. Break candied bacon into pieces or slice into thin strips; arrange on top of frosted cupcakes.

CANDIED BACON

This typically savory food gets a sweet treatment: it's coated in cocoa powder and brown sugar and baked until crispy and caramelized. Eat it as a snack or throw it into your next batch of cookie batter or caramel corn—you'll never look at bacon the same way again. *Makes 4 strips. Total time: 45 minutes.*

3 tablespoons light brown sugar, packed

1 teaspoon cocoa powder

4 strips bacon

1. Preheat oven to 375°F. Line a baking sheet with aluminum foil; set an ovenproof wire baking rack on top of foil and lightly grease with cooking spray.

2. In a shallow dish, whisk together brown sugar and cocoa powder until evenly distributed. Press bacon into sugar mixture to coat, shaking off excess.

3. Arrange bacon on prepared rack, leaving plenty of space between slices. Bake for 30 to 40 minutes, flipping every 10 minutes, until bacon is browned and crisp. Remove from oven and let cool completely.

MOCHA ICE CREAM

Because this mocha ice cream is made with whole coffee beans, you can use your favorite roast. Try decaf beans for an indulgent treat that won't keep you up at night. *Makes 1 quart. Active time: 30 minutes. Total time: 4 hours.*

---

³/₄ cup granulated sugar

2 tablespoons cocoa powder

Pinch salt

3 cups half-and-half, divided

1¹/₂ cups whole coffee beans (regular or decaf)

4 large egg yolks

¹/₂ teaspoon pure vanilla extract

1. In a medium saucepan, whisk together sugar, cocoa powder, and salt. Whisk in 2 cups of the half-and-half and stir over medium heat until mixture just starts to steam. Remove from heat and stir in coffee beans; cover and let steep for 1 hour.

2. Pour the remaining 1 cup half-and-half into a medium heatproof bowl and nest it inside a larger bowl of ice water.

3. Return saucepan to medium heat until mixture just starts to steam. In a medium bowl, whisk egg yolks. Slowly whisk in about half of the warm coffee mixture, ¹/₃ cup at a time, until warm to the touch. (Do this gradually to temper the egg yolks rather than cook them.)

4. Pour tempered egg mixture into saucepan and return to medium heat. Stir constantly until it thickens slightly and coats the back of a spatula, about 5 to 7 minutes; the temperature should be 165°F to 170°F (don't let it boil). Pour mixture through a fine-mesh sieve into the nested bowl of chilled half-and-half, discarding coffee beans and any solids. Add vanilla extract and stir until cool.

5. Cover with plastic wrap, carefully pressing plastic onto the surface of the cream mixture to prevent a skin from forming. Refrigerate until completely cool, at least 3 hours but preferably overnight. Churn according to manufacturer's instructions, then transfer to a freezer-safe container and freeze until firm.

a heavenly pair

MOCHA ICE CREAM PIE WITH BISCOTTI CRUST

makes 8 servings ★ active time: 1 hour ★ total time: 5 to 8 hours

We've amped up your midmorning mocha with a subzero twist. It may just
be your new favorite way to enjoy coffee and biscotti—no dipping necessary.

For Biscotti Crust
1½ cups finely crushed biscotti*
(about 7 ounces)
5 tablespoons unsalted butter, melted

1 quart store-bought or homemade
mocha ice cream (see page 111)

For Topping
Whipped cream
Chocolate shavings
Chopped toasted almonds

*Biscotti are dry, crunchy Italian
cookies. Look for them in the bakery
department or cookie aisle in major
grocery stores or specialty Italian food
stores. Substitute chocolate or vanilla
wafers if you can't find them.

1. To prepare the crust, mix biscotti crumbs and melted butter with a fork
until evenly moistened and mixture has the consistency of wet sand. Firmly
press into the bottom and up the sides of a 9-inch pie dish. Freeze for at
least 30 minutes or until ready to use.

2. If using store-bought ice cream, let soften at room temperature until it is
the consistency of soft-serve. Freshly churned homemade ice cream is the
perfect consistency right out of the machine.

3. Spread ice cream into prepared crust. Cover with plastic wrap and
freeze until completely firm, at least 4 hours.

4. To serve pie, run a knife under hot water for 30 seconds before cutting
into slices. Top with a dollop of whipped cream and a sprinkle of chocolate
shavings and chopped almonds.

★ ★ ★

Chocolate Shavings Made Easy

To make chocolate shavings, heat a dark or semisweet
chocolate bar in the microwave for a few seconds on medium
power until just barely softened. Then run a vegetable peeler
along the edge of the bar.

summer in a glass

GRAPEFRUIT HERB SODAS

makes 4 servings ★ active time: 5 minutes ★ total time: 15 minutes

As refreshing as a summer breeze, this homemade soda is the perfect thirst-quencher for your next picnic or barbecue. We like it best with thyme, basil, or mint, but feel free to experiment and find your own favorite herbal combination.

½ cup granulated sugar

A few sprigs fresh thyme, basil, or mint, or the fresh herb of your choice

½ cup freshly squeezed grapefruit juice

2 cups club soda

1. In a small saucepan, combine sugar with ½ cup water. Bring to a simmer over medium heat, stirring until sugar is dissolved. Remove from heat; add herbs, cover, and let steep for 10 minutes. Remove herbs and let cool completely.

2. Fill four 8-ounce glasses with ice. Pour grapefruit juice over ice; stir in 1 to 2 tablespoons of the herbed sugar syrup (or more to taste). Top with soda.

For the Adult Set

★ **Spiked Grapefruit Herb Sodas:** Add a splash of your favorite liquor (try gin, vodka, or light rum).

tiny, tart, tasty

⇒ LEMON POPPY SEED THUMBPRINTS ⇐

makes 40 cookies ★ active time: 30 minutes ★ total time: 3 hours

Reminiscent of lemon poppy seed muffins, these delicate little cookies are the perfect combination of sweet and sour, cute and elegant; they're tender and buttery with a rich Meyer lemon curd and a hint of nuttiness from the poppy seeds.

For Curd

1 large egg

1 large egg yolk

1/4 cup granulated sugar

1/4 cup Meyer lemon juice*

1/2 teaspoon finely grated Meyer lemon zest

2 tablespoons unsalted butter, cut into cubes

1/2 teaspoon poppy seeds

For Cookies

1 cup (2 sticks) unsalted butter, room temperature

2/3 cup granulated sugar

2 large egg yolks

1 teaspoon pure vanilla extract

2 cups all-purpose flour

1/2 teaspoon salt

*Meyer lemons are a cross between lemons and mandarin oranges; they have a sweeter flavor and a darker color than regular lemons. You can use regular lemons in this recipe, but increase the sugar to 1/3 cup to offset the tartness.

1. To prepare curd, whisk together egg, egg yolk, sugar, lemon juice, and lemon zest in a glass or stainless-steel heatproof bowl. Place bowl over a pot of gently simmering water and cook, whisking constantly, until mixture thickens enough to coat the back of a spoon (it should reach approximately 165ºF), about 5 to 7 minutes. Do not let it boil.

2. Strain mixture through a fine-mesh sieve. Whisk in butter until melted and smooth. Stir in poppy seeds. Cover with plastic wrap, pressing plastic onto the surface of the curd to prevent a skin from forming. Refrigerate until set and thoroughly chilled, at least 2 hours.

3. For cookies, preheat oven to 375ºF and line a baking sheet with parchment paper. Beat together butter and sugar with an electric mixer on medium-high speed until light and fluffy, about 2 to 3 minutes. Beat in egg yolks and vanilla extract. Add flour and salt and mix until incorporated and dough comes together in a ball.

4. Form dough into 1-inch balls and arrange on prepared baking sheet. Flatten balls slightly with your thumb or the back of a small spoon, leaving an indentation in the center.

5. Bake cookies for 10 minutes. Remove baking sheet from oven. If indentations look shallow, further define them with the back of a spoon and then fill each with approximately 1/2 teaspoon curd. Bake for an additional 3 to 4 minutes, or until curd is set and edges of cookies are lightly golden. Transfer cookies to wire racks to cool.

★ ★ ★

The Possibilities Are Endless

These shortbread thumbprints go great with lemon curd but are also delicious filled with strawberry or other preserves, or even chocolate-hazelnut spread.

a traditional cocktail infused with bacon

BACON OLD-FASHIONEDS

makes 2 servings ★ *total time: 5 minutes*

The old-fashioned is a classic whiskey cocktail dating back to the 1880s. But there's nothing ordinary about this new-fashioned drink, made by infusing bourbon with smoky bacon flavor and replacing the classic sugar cube with pure maple syrup.

½ cup bacon-infused bourbon (page 120)

Orange bitters*

1 to 2 teaspoons pure maple syrup, divided

For Garnish

Orange peel (optional)

2 slices cooked bacon (optional)

*Made from a distillation of aromatic herbs, flowers, and plants, bitters typically have a high alcohol content and taste bittersweet. They've long been used as digestive aids, hangover cures, and the secret ingredient in many cocktails. You can find bitters at liquor stores or online.

Fill two lowball glasses with ice. Divide bacon-infused bourbon evenly between the glasses, and then stir in 2 to 3 dashes bitters and ½ to 1 teaspoon maple syrup to each glass. Garnish with orange peel and bacon slices, if desired.

A Lightweight Version

For a bubblier, less potent cocktail, add a splash of soda water to the final drink.

BACON-INFUSED BOURBON

Making a bacon cocktail involves a bit of trickery: You want to get the bacon flavor into the booze without a greasy mess. But it's easier than you think, and best of all, you don't have to waste any bacon to do it. All you need is the leftover fat. *Makes ½ cup. Active time: 20 minutes. Total time: 8 hours.*

2 slices thick-cut, smoky bacon

½ cup bourbon

1. Cook bacon in a skillet over medium heat until fat is rendered. Be careful not to overcook bacon, as it will impart a burnt flavor. Reserve bacon for garnish or for another use. Let fat cool in skillet for about 15 minutes; place a coffee filter inside a fine-mesh sieve. Pour cooled fat through sieve into a heatproof bowl.

2. In a half-pint or larger glass jar with a tight-fiting lid, mix 1 tablespoon bacon fat with bourbon. Close tightly and gently shake to combine. Let stand at room temperature for 4 to 6 hours, then freeze until fat solidifies and rises to the top, 1 to 2 hours.

3. Spoon off as much of the solidified fat as you can, then pour liquid through another coffee-filter-lined sieve to remove any remaining solids.

Bourbon can be infused with other flavors as well. Try fruits like apples or peaches or spices, such as vanilla beans or cinnamon sticks or even dried chili peppers. Combine the bourbon with your flavoring in a glass mason jar and refrigerate for 2 to 4 days, shaking occasionally. When you've achieved the desired flavor, strain bourbon through a fine-mesh sieve into a clean jar.

HOW TO INFUSE BOURBON WITH BACON

1. Place a coffee filter inside a fine-mesh sieve. Pour cooled bacon fat through sieve into a half-pint or larger glass jar that seals with a tight-fitting lid. Close tightly and shake gently to combine.

2. Let stand at room temperature for 4 to 6 hours, then freeze for 1 to 2 hours or refrigerate overnight, until fat solidifies and rises to the top. Spoon off as much fat as you can.

3. Pour bourbon through another coffee-filter-lined sieve to remove remaining solids. Transfer to a clean jar and store in the refrigerator or freezer for up to a month.

a bright and fruity frozen cocktail

BLOOD ORANGE MIMOSA SORBET

makes about 1 quart ★ active time: 30 minutes ★ total time: 5 hours

The beloved brunch cocktail gets an after-dinner twist thanks to rosy-red blood orange juice and champagne, frozen together in a sweet and icy treat.

2½ cups blood orange juice (bottled or freshly squeezed from 15 to 16 blood oranges)

1 cup champagne or sparkling white wine

¾ cup granulated sugar

3 tablespoons corn syrup

1. Stir together all ingredients in a saucepan over medium-high heat until sugar is dissolved. Transfer to a heatproof bowl; cover and refrigerate until completely chilled, at least 2 hours or overnight.

2. Pour mixture into an ice-cream machine and churn according to manufacturer's instructions until it reaches the consistency of thick slush. Transfer to a freezer-safe container and freeze until firm, at least 2 hours.

★ ★ ★

Blood oranges have a short season—they are typically available in grocery stores from December through March. If you can't find them, substitute regular oranges to make a classic mimosa sorbet.

two cocktails in one

🍴 FROZEN SUNRISE MARGARITAS 🍴

makes 4 drinks ★ total time: 10 minutes

The tequila sunrise and the margarita come together in this frozen drink recipe
that's bursting with citrus notes and a refreshing tang.

Margarita or coarse sea salt,
for rimming glass

1 lime wedge, for rimming glass

½ cup frozen orange juice
concentrate

1½ cups orange juice

¾ cup (6 ounces) tequila

2 tablespoons (1 ounce) Cointreau
or triple sec

2 tablespoons lime juice

3 cups crushed ice

¼ cup grenadine

For Garnish
4 orange slices
4 maraschino cherries

1. Spread a layer of salt in a shallow dish. Run lime wedge around the rims of 4 highball glasses to moisten; dip rims in salt.

2. Place orange juice concentrate, orange juice, tequila, Cointreau, and lime juice in a blender. Add ice and pulse until smooth. Divide margarita evenly among glasses.

3. Tilt glasses and pour 1 tablespoon grenadine down the side of each drink; grenadine will sink to the bottom and create a sunset effect. Garnish with orange slices and maraschino cherries and serve.

★ ★ ★

*The straight sides of highball glasses are ideal for
achieving the sunrise effect. Traditional margarita
glasses won't work if you want this look.*

breakfast deliciousness baked up just right

⊨ ✦ GRANOLA COOKIES ✦ ⊨

makes about 40 cookies ★ active time: 20 minutes ★ total time: 1 hour

Everything you love about granola is baked right into this salty-sweet oatmeal cookie that has plenty of chew, a bit of crunch, and a hearty dose of chocolate. These cookies make a fabulous afternoon snack on their own or a decadent dessert treat when served with vanilla ice cream sandwiched between them.

2¼ cups all-purpose flour

1 teaspoon salt

1 teaspoon baking powder

½ teaspoon baking soda

1 cup (2 sticks) unsalted butter, room temperature

1¼ cups light brown sugar, packed

¾ cup granulated sugar

2 large eggs

1½ teaspoons pure vanilla extract

2 cups plain granola*

½ cup old-fashioned rolled oats

1 cup semisweet chocolate chips

½ cup dried cherries, coarsely chopped

*We recommend using a simple granola containing just nuts and oats in this recipe. Use your favorite or try ours (see page 128), which is easy to prepare.

1. Preheat oven to 350°F; line a baking sheet with parchment paper. Sift together flour, salt, baking powder, and baking soda into a bowl; set aside.

2. In a large mixing bowl or the bowl of a stand mixer, beat butter and sugars on medium-high speed until light and fluffy, 1 to 2 minutes. Mix in eggs and vanilla and beat until smooth.

3. With mixer on low speed, add flour mixture until well incorporated. Stir in granola and oats, followed by chocolate chips and dried cherries.

4. Drop dough by the rounded tablespoonful onto prepared baking sheet, leaving about 2 inches in between. Bake for 12 to 14 minutes, or until cookies are puffed and edges are lightly golden. Let cookies cool on baking sheets for 5 minutes, then transfer to wire racks to cool completely.

BASIC GRANOLA

This all-purpose granola recipe couldn't be easier. If you plan to use it in Granola Cookies (page 126), we recommend keeping the flavors simple and the mix-ins to a minimum. But feel free to adjust the types of nuts and amount of coconut to your liking and mix in raisins, dried cherries, or other dried fruit after baking, if desired. *Makes about 8 cups. Active time: 15 minutes. Total time: 45 minutes.*

4 cups old-fashioned rolled oats

1 cup shelled sunflower seeds

1 cup unsweetened shredded coconut

1 cup roughly chopped mixed nuts (almonds, pecans, cashews, etc.)

¼ teaspoon salt

¾ cup honey

¼ cup canola oil

1 teaspoon pure vanilla extract

1. Preheat oven to 325°F. Line a baking sheet with aluminum foil; spray lightly with cooking spray.

2. In a large mixing bowl, stir together oats, sunflower seeds, coconut, nuts, and salt.

3. In a heatproof bowl or glass measuring cup, microwave honey, oil, and vanilla extract on high power until mixture is hot and bubbling, about 45 seconds. Pour over dry ingredients and toss to coat.

4. Spread granola onto prepared baking sheet in an even layer. Bake, stirring every 15 minutes, until granola is golden brown and fragrant, 30 to 45 minutes. Let cool, stirring occasionally to break up the large pieces. Stored in an airtight container, granola will keep for up to 4 weeks.

SIMPLE SWEET CREPES

This is a basic sweet crepe recipe that can be used for the Bananas Foster Crepe Cake (page 130), or paired with a variety of other sweet fillings, including fruit preserves or fresh fruit, chocolate chips, honey and ricotta cheese, or peanut butter. *Makes about 20 6-inch crepes. Total time: 1 hour 15 minutes.*

1½ cups all-purpose flour

¼ cup granulated sugar

¼ teaspoon salt

2 cups whole milk

4 eggs

5 tablespoons unsalted butter, melted and cooled to room temperature, plus more for skillet

½ teaspoon pure vanilla extract

1. Combine all ingredients in a blender. Mix on medium speed for 10 to 15 seconds, or until mixture is smooth and uniform, with the consistency of heavy cream; if it is too thick or too thin, mix in a bit more milk or flour, respectively. Pour into a bowl and refrigerate for at least 30 minutes and up to 1 hour.

2. Heat a 6-inch-diameter nonstick skillet over medium heat. Brush with melted butter.

3. Ladle 2 to 3 tablespoons of batter onto the center of skillet; tilt pan to swirl batter evenly around pan and form a thin, uniform layer. Cook for 1 to 2 minutes, or until bottom is lightly golden brown. With a large thin spatula, carefully flip the crepe and cook for another minute. Transfer to a platter or baking sheet to cool. Repeat with remaining batter.

★ ★ ★

See How It's Done

Flip to pages 44 and 45 for a savory whole wheat crepe recipe and more tips and photos.

a stunning no-bake confection

⚞ BANANAS FOSTER CREPE CAKE ⚟

makes one 6-inch cake ★ active time: 2 hours ★ total time: 24 hours

Forget two- or three-layer cakes—how about a twenty-layer cake? Sometimes called a *mille crêpe* cake, or "cake of a thousand layers," this gorgeous no-bake confection stacks thin, lacy crepes and a creamy bananas Foster pudding. It's topped with even more caramelized banana goodness to create a truly impressive dessert.

For Filling

3 tablespoons unsalted butter

1/3 cup plus 3 tablespoons light brown sugar, packed and divided

1/4 teaspoon ground cinnamon

2 bananas, peeled and sliced

1 1/2 tablespoons rum

1/4 cup cornstarch

1/4 teaspoon salt

2 1/4 cups whole milk

4 large egg yolks

3/4 teaspoon pure vanilla extract

About 20 6-inch crepes (page 129)

For Topping

2 tablespoons unsalted butter

2 tablespoons light brown sugar, packed

1/8 teaspoon ground cinnamon

1 banana, sliced on the diagonal

1 tablespoon rum

1. For the filling, melt butter with 3 tablespoons of the brown sugar and cinnamon in a skillet over medium heat. When butter is melted and sugar is dissolved, stir in banana slices. Cook for 8 to 10 minutes, or until bananas are softened and beginning to brown. Stir in rum and cook for 1 to 2 minutes more. Let cool to lukewarm; mash with a fork or potato masher.

2. In a saucepan, whisk together the remaining 1/3 cup brown sugar, cornstarch, and salt. Whisk in milk and cook over medium heat, continuing to whisk, until mixture begins to thicken and just starts to bubble, about 5 to 7 minutes.

3. In a small bowl, whisk egg yolks. Slowly whisk in some of the warm milk mixture, 1/4 cup at a time, until about half of milk mixture has been incorporated and yolk mixture is warm to the touch. You want to do this gradually, so you temper the egg yolks rather than cook them. Pour yolk mixture back into the saucepan and return to medium heat, stirring constantly, until thick, 2 to 3 minutes more. Stir in mashed banana mixture and vanilla extract. Press pudding through a fine-mesh sieve to remove any lumps; cover and refrigerate until completely cool, at least 1 hour.

4. Place 1 crepe on a plate or serving dish. Spread a thin layer (about 1 1/2 tablespoons) of the filling on top. Top with another crepe. Continue layering filling and crepes until you run out, ending with a crepe on top. Refrigerate until set, at least 4 hours but preferably overnight.

5. Just before serving, prepare topping: combine butter, brown sugar, and cinnamon in a skillet over medium heat. When butter is melted and sugar is dissolved, add banana slices. Cook for 8 to 10 minutes, or until bananas are softened and beginning to brown. Add rum and cook for 1 to 2 minutes more. Arrange banana slices on top of cake; pour remaining caramel sauce over top.

Italian espresso and ice cream treat

AFFOGATO AL CAFFÈ

makes 1 serving ★ *total time: 5 minutes*

Affogato means "drowned" in Italian, and this traditional Italian dessert is just that: a scoop of gelato or ice cream drowning in espresso. It's an after-dinner drink and dessert all in one.

½ cup (1 large scoop) vanilla gelato or premium vanilla ice cream 2 ounces (¼ cup) freshly brewed espresso	Place ice cream in a dessert bowl or mug. Pour hot espresso over top and serve.

More to Try

★ **Mocha Affogato:** Substitute chocolate gelato for vanilla. Drizzle with hot fudge sauce.

★ **Caramel Affogato:** Drizzle with 2 tablespoons of caramel topping.

★ **Tipsy Affogato:** Stir 1 ounce of your favorite cream liqueur or amaretto into hot espresso.

★ **Cocoa Affogato:** Replace espresso with hot chocolate. Top with whipped cream.

chocolate peanut butter glazed

BANANA BREAD BUNDT CAKE

makes 12 to 16 servings ★ *active time: 30 minutes* ★ *total time: 1 hour 30 minutes*

Our family strongly believes in eating chocolate for breakfast. Our tried-and-true banana bread recipe is chock-full of chocolate chips, making this decadent quick bread practically a cake. That "almost cake" recipe inspired this actual cake, complete with a luscious chocolate peanut butter glaze.

For Cake

2½ cups all-purpose flour

1 teaspoon baking powder

½ teaspoon baking soda

½ teaspoon salt

1 cup granulated sugar

¾ cup (1½ sticks) unsalted butter, room temperature

2 large eggs, room temperature

3 very ripe bananas, mashed (about 1¼ cups mashed)

1 teaspoon pure vanilla extract

½ cup whole milk

1 cup semisweet chocolate chips

For Glaze

3 ounces (½ cup) semisweet chocolate chips*

⅓ cup heavy cream

2 tablespoons creamy peanut butter

*Be sure to use semisweet chocolate, not dark or bittersweet, which will make the glaze bitter.

1. Preheat oven to 350°F. Generously butter a standard (12-cup) Bundt pan, making sure to get in all the nooks and crannies. Dust with flour, tapping out any excess.

2. In a bowl, sift together flour, baking powder, baking soda, and salt.

3. In a large mixing bowl or the bowl of a stand mixer, beat sugar and butter on medium speed until fluffy, 1 to 2 minutes. Add eggs, 1 at a time, mixing well after each addition. Scrape down the sides of the bowl, then mix in mashed banana and vanilla. Add dry ingredients in three additions, alternating with two additions of milk, mixing until incorporated. Fold in chocolate chips.

4. Pour batter into prepared pan. Bake for 40 to 50 minutes, or until a toothpick inserted in the deepest part of the pan comes out clean. Place pan on a wire rack to cool. When pan is cool enough to handle, invert pan over wire rack; cake should come out cleanly.

5. To prepare glaze, warm chocolate and cream in a small saucepan over low heat until melted. Add peanut butter and stir until smooth. Let cool until glaze has thickened slightly (it should be pourable but not runny), then pour over cake. Refrigerate glazed cake in an airtight container for up to 3 days until ready to serve.

a creamy, fruity dessert

WHITE CHOCOLATE & BLUEBERRY TART

makes 6 to 8 servings ★ active time: 30 minutes ★ total time: 3 hours 30 minutes

Fresh fruit is a breakfast staple, but for dessert it is often passed over for darker indulgences like chocolates and caramels. This delightful no-bake tart is sure to satisfy. It boasts a delicate white chocolate mousse filling that is a perfect counterpart to the brightness of fresh blueberries. A layer of preserves packs in even more berry flavor.

For Crust
5 tablespoons unsalted butter

1 ounce white chocolate, chopped

1½ cups (8 ounces) vanilla wafer crumbs

For Filling
1 teaspoon lemon juice

1 teaspoon unflavored gelatin

6 ounces white chocolate, chopped

1¼ cups heavy cream, divided

½ cup blueberry preserves

1 pint fresh blueberries

★ ★ ★

No food processor? No worries. Very finely chop the white chocolate and place it in a heatproof bowl. Pour the warm cream mixture over top and stir until smooth, as if you were making ganache.

1. In a microwave-safe bowl, microwave butter and white chocolate on high power for about 30 seconds, stirring until melted and smooth. Combine with cookie crumbs in a large bowl and stir until evenly moistened. Press into a 4.5-by-14-inch rectangular tart pan or a 9.5-inch round tart pan with a removable bottom. Freeze for at least 1 hour, or until set.

2. To prepare filling, combine lemon juice with 2 tablespoons water in a small bowl. Sprinkle gelatin on top and let stand for 5 minutes.

3. Place white chocolate in the bowl of a food processor; pulse until finely chopped.

4. Heat ½ cup of the cream in a small saucepan over medium heat until it just starts to simmer. Remove from heat and stir in gelatin mixture. Pour mixture into food processor with white chocolate and pulse 2 to 3 times, or until smooth. Transfer mixture to a bowl; cover and chill for no more than 15 to 20 minutes, until cooled completely but not yet firm.

5. Whip the remaining ¾ cup cream until it forms soft peaks. Fold whipped cream into chilled gelatin mixture until smooth. If your gelatin mixture got too firm and made the mousse slightly lumpy, press it through a fine-mesh sieve with a spatula to remove any lumps.

6. Remove crust from freezer and spread a thin layer of blueberry preserves in the bottom. Pour white chocolate mousse into crust, smoothing out the top with an offset spatula. Refrigerate for 15 minutes, then sprinkle blueberries over top. Chill for 1 to 2 hours, or until completely set, then slice and serve. Covered in the refrigerator, tart will keep for up to 3 days.

dark and rich

CHOCOLATE BROWNIE WAFFLES WITH BLACKBERRY SAUCE

makes 4 to 6 waffles ★ active time: 30 minutes ★ total time: 45 minutes

These chocolaty cakelike waffles come together even quicker than cupcakes. Tangy blackberry sauce and a dollop of whipped cream add the perfect finishing touch.

For Blackberry Sauce
2 cups (10 ounces) fresh or frozen blackberries

2 tablespoons granulated sugar

Juice from 1 lemon

For Waffles
½ cup unsalted butter, cut into cubes

3 ounces dark chocolate, chopped

¾ cup granulated sugar

2 large eggs, room temperature

1 teaspoon pure vanilla extract

½ cup whole milk

1 cup all-purpose flour

2 tablespoons cocoa powder

2 teaspoons baking powder

½ teaspoon salt

Freshly whipped cream, for topping

1. To prepare blackberry sauce, stir together blackberries, sugar, and lemon juice in a small saucepan over medium heat; if using fresh blackberries, add 2 tablespoons water. Bring to a simmer, stirring and crushing berries with the back of a wooden spoon. Simmer for 5 to 7 minutes, or until sugar is dissolved and berries begin to break down. Transfer to a blender or food processor and pulse until smooth. Press through a fine mesh sieve to remove seeds. Sauce can be made a day ahead and refrigerated in an airtight container; warm in a saucepan over low heat prior to serving.

2. For waffles, in a saucepan or a double boiler over low heat, stir butter and chocolate until melted and smooth. Remove from heat and stir in sugar. Whisk in eggs and vanilla, followed by milk. Stir in flour, cocoa powder, baking powder, and salt until just incorporated.

3. Preheat a Belgian waffle iron according to manufacturer's instructions. Drop about ½ cup batter onto iron for each waffle (more or less depending on the size of your iron), and cook until outside is crispy. Serve warm, drizzled with blackberry sauce and topped with more blackberries and freshly whipped cream, if desired.

Coconut Brownie Waffles

For a lighter version with a subtle coconut flavor, replace the butter with coconut oil (found in the natural-foods section of major grocery stores or at health-food stores) and the milk with coconut milk.

FRUIT SALAD SANGRIA

makes 8 servings ★ active time: 15 minutes ★ total time: 4 hours

Sangria is the perfect refreshment on a hot summer day. This recipe combines the best of spring *and* summer: sweet ripe strawberries and succulent peaches, plus elderflower liqueur for a unique floral character. It's essential to make the sangria ahead of time to allow the flavors to fully develop.

1 (750-milliliter) bottle moscato

4 ounces strawberries, hulled and halved (about ¾ cup)

1 orange, thinly sliced

1 peach, pitted and sliced

½ cup freshly squeezed orange juice (from 1 large orange)

2 ounces (¼ cup) elderflower liqueur (such as St-Germain)

2 tablespoons freshly squeezed lemon juice (from 1 large lemon)

16 ounces (2 cups) soda water or club soda

Combine wine, strawberries, oranges, peaches, orange juice, liqueur, and lemon juice in a large pitcher. Refrigerate for at least 4 hours or overnight. To serve, pour over ice and top each drink with a splash of soda water.

Moscato is a sweet, fruity wine available in both white and red varieties. Either would work beautifully in this sangria, or feel free to use your favorite fruity white wine instead. You may want to add a dash of simple syrup to enhance the sweetness.

tall on flavor

✦ STRAWBERRY & BASIL SHORTCAKES ✦

makes 8 shortcakes ★ active time: 20 minutes ★ total time: 1 hour

These rustic shortcakes are inspired by caprese salad, a simple Italian dish made up of mozzarella, tomatoes, and basil drizzled with balsamic vinegar. Don't worry, we're not trying to turn tomatoes into dessert. These shortcakes layer balsamic-roasted strawberries, whipped cream, and basil atop a light and flaky cream biscuit.

For Cream Biscuits

2 cups all-purpose flour

2 tablespoons granulated sugar

1 tablespoon baking powder

$\frac{1}{2}$ teaspoon salt

6 tablespoons cold unsalted butter, cut into cubes

1 cup heavy cream, plus more for brushing

Turbinado sugar,* for sprinkling

For Filling

$1\frac{1}{2}$ pounds fresh strawberries, hulled and halved (quartered if large)

3 tablespoons balsamic vinegar

$1\frac{1}{2}$ tablespoons extra-virgin olive oil

$1\frac{1}{2}$ tablespoons honey

1 cup heavy cream

2 tablespoons confectioners' sugar

Small handful fresh basil, cut into thin strips

*Turbinado sugar, also called raw, natural, or demerara sugar, is a coarse, light brown sugar. It gives these biscuits a fantastic crunch that finer granulated sugar couldn't.

1. Preheat oven to 350°F.

2. In a large bowl, whisk together flour, sugar, baking powder, and salt. Using a pastry blender or fork, cut butter into dry ingredients until mixture resembles coarse crumbs. Stir in cream with a fork until mixture is evenly moistened.

3. Gather dough and turn it out onto a lightly floured surface, kneading to incorporate any loose crumbs but taking care not to overwork it. Press into a $\frac{1}{2}$-inch-thick round. Cut into $3\frac{1}{2}$-inch circles using a biscuit cutter or the open end of a round drinking glass. Transfer biscuits to a baking sheet; brush with cream and sprinkle with turbinado sugar. Bake for 18 to 20 minutes, or until tops are lightly golden.

4. Line a large rimmed baking sheet with parchment paper or aluminum foil; brush with oil or spray with cooking spray.

5. Toss strawberries with vinegar, oil, and honey. Pour onto prepared baking sheet and spread in a single layer. Bake for 25 to 30 minutes, or until berries are soft and juices are thickened but not burned.

6. Combine cream and confectioners' sugar in large bowl and whisk vigorously by hand or with an electric mixer until cream forms soft peaks.

7. Carefully split biscuits in half. Spoon roasted berries onto the bottom of each biscuit; top with a generous dollop of whipped cream and a sprinkle of basil. Replace tops of biscuits and serve warm or at room temperature.

⥇ VIETNAMESE ICED-COFFEE POPS ⥇

makes 6 pops ★ active time: 10 minutes ★ total time: 5 hours

Vietnamese iced coffee is a traditional French/Vietnamese beverage made from strong, slow-drip coffee served with sweetened condensed milk over ice. It's incredibly rich and refreshing; the only way to make it more so is to freeze it in a pop mold.

1½ cups (12 ounces) strong brewed coffee

½ cup sweetened condensed milk

Stir hot coffee into sweetened condensed milk to incorporate. Refrigerate until completely cool, at least 1 hour, then pour into pop molds. Insert sticks and freeze until solid, at least 4 hours or overnight. To unmold, run under warm water until pops slide out cleanly.

★ ★ ★

Although chicory coffee (such as Café du Monde)
is commonly used in Vietnamese iced coffee, any
dark roast will work, as will decaf.

⇥ EARL GREY PANNA COTTA ⇤

makes 6 servings ★ active time: 15 minutes ★ total time: 4 hours

Do you have your morning tea with milk or lemon? This dessert brings them all together in a sweet and jiggly custard. Panna cotta (which translates literally as "boiled cream," although it's not really boiled) is an Italian gelatinized custard that is impressive any way you serve it: in teacups to hint at the flavors infused within, or in more traditional ramekins or panna cotta molds.

1 packet unflavored gelatin

2 cups half-and-half

1/3 cup granulated sugar

2 bags Earl Grey tea

Peel from 1 lemon*

*Use a vegetable peeler to remove large strips of the lemon peel.

1. In a small bowl, sprinkle gelatin over 1/4 cup cold water; let sit until softened, about 5 minutes.

2. Heat half-and-half and sugar in a medium saucepan over medium heat until sugar is dissolved and mixture just starts to steam (do not let it boil); remove from heat. Submerge tea bags and lemon peel in mixture; cover and steep for 5 minutes.

3. Remove lemon peel and tea bags, squeezing out any remaining liquid from the bags before discarding.

4. Stir gelatin into warm tea mixture until dissolved (if tea mixture has sat for more than 5 minutes, warm over medium heat until liquid just starts to steam again and then stir in gelatin). Pour into teacups or ramekins; chill uncovered until set, at least 4 hours.

soda fountain style

CHOCOLATE MAPLE FUDGE SAUCE

makes 1½ cups ★ active time: 15 minutes ★ total time: 30 minutes

Inspired by Lindsay's Grandma Bettie's recipe, this twist on a soda-fountain favorite infuses classic hot fudge sauce with pure maple syrup. It's great served warm over ice cream or pancakes.

1 cup granulated sugar

⅓ cup cocoa powder

2 tablespoons all-purpose flour

¼ teaspoon salt

¼ cup pure maple syrup

1 tablespoon unsalted butter

½ teaspoon pure vanilla extract

⅛ teaspoon pure maple extract*

*For classic fudge sauce, omit maple extract and use corn syrup in place of maple syrup.

1. Sift together sugar, cocoa powder, flour, and salt in a medium saucepan. Whisk in 1 cup boiling water, maple syrup, and butter. Bring to a boil over medium heat, whisking occasionally; simmer for 7 to 8 minutes, or until thickened slightly and reduced by half.

2. Remove from heat and transfer to a heatproof bowl; stir in vanilla and maple extracts. Let cool to room temperature, stirring occasionally, about 20 minutes (don't refrigerate the sauce before it has completely cooled or it may become grainy).

3. When completely cooled, transfer sauce to a glass jar or airtight container and refrigerate for up to 2 weeks. Warm gently in the microwave before serving.

happiness is rainbow sprinkles

DOUGHNUT FUDGE SUNDAES

makes 2 sundaes ★ total time: 2 minutes

To doughnut or not to doughnut: is it even a question? This extra-decadent and ultra-simple sundae takes an ordinary glazed doughnut and tops it with a heaping scoop of ice cream, maple hot fudge sauce, and all the toppings your heart desires.

2 maple or chocolate glazed doughnuts (with sprinkles!)

2 large scoops vanilla, chocolate, or mocha ice cream*

¼ cup Chocolate Maple Fudge Sauce**

Sprinkles, nuts, or other additional toppings, as desired

Whipped cream, for topping

2 maraschino cherries

*Store-bought is fine, or see page 111 for homemade mocha ice cream recipe.

**Store-bought chocolate sauce can be used, but the chocolate maple sauce on page 149 is delicious.

1. Place each doughnut in a serving dish and top with a scoop of ice cream.

2. Warm fudge sauce in the microwave for 5 to 10 seconds on high power, then generously drizzle over ice cream. Garnish with toppings, a dollop of whipped cream, and a cherry on top.

Additional toppings include rainbow sprinkles, mini semisweet or white chocolate chips, toffee baking bits, caramel sauce, melted strawberry jam, chopped nuts, or even crumbled bits of candied bacon (page 110).

ice cream and pancakes—together at last

MINT CHOCOLATE CHIP PANCAKES

makes 12 pancakes (3 to 4 servings) ★ *total time: 30 minutes*

There's nothing as delightful as a towering stack of fluffy pancakes. Unless those pancakes happen to be reminiscent of your favorite mint chocolate chip ice cream. The green food coloring here is optional but adds nicely to the appeal.

1⅓ cup all-purpose flour

1 tablespoon granulated sugar

1 teaspoon baking powder

½ teaspoon baking soda

½ teaspoon salt

1 cup buttermilk

1 large egg

2 tablespoons butter, melted and cooled to lukewarm, plus more for cooking

½ teaspoon pure vanilla extract

½ teaspoon pure mint extract*

3 to 4 drops green food coloring (optional)

¾ cup mini semisweet chocolate chips, plus more for topping

Whipped cream, for serving

Vanilla ice cream, for serving

Store-bought or homemade hot fudge sauce (page 149), for serving

*Mint and peppermint extracts are similar but not identical in flavor. Mint extract typically contains both peppermint and spearmint, whereas pure peppermint is popular in holiday treats like candy canes. Use whichever minty extract you prefer.

1. Sift together flour, sugar, baking powder, baking soda, and salt into a bowl.

2. Whisk together buttermilk, egg, butter, extracts, and food coloring (if using) in a small bowl. Add to dry ingredients and stir until incorporated. Stir in chocolate chips.

3. Heat a large nonstick skillet or griddle over medium heat. Add ½ tablespoon butter; it should sizzle and melt almost immediately. Ladle ¼ cup of pancake batter into skillet for each pancake, taking care not to let the pancakes run together. Cook for 1 to 2 minutes, until bottom is golden brown and edges begin to bubble, then carefully flip and cook for 1 to 2 minutes more. Transfer to plates. Repeat with remaining batter.

4. Serve warm with whipped cream, vanilla ice cream, hot fudge sauce, and more chocolate chips, if desired.

★ ★ ★

Pancakes Inspired by Ice Creams

★ **Candy Cane Pancakes:** Replace mint extract with peppermint extract. Add ¼ cup finely chopped candy canes along with or in place of chocolate chips. Use red food coloring instead of green.

★ **Almond Chip Pancakes:** Replace mint extract with almond extract. Add ¼ cup chopped almonds to batter. Omit food coloring.

★ **Plain Old Chocolate Chip Pancakes:** Omit mint extract and increase vanilla extract to 1 teaspoon; omit food coloring.

to breakfast lovers everywhere

THANK YOU

This book didn't magically appear from the depths of our kitchen. It is a result of the time and effort of many people, and we are forever grateful to all of them. Thank you to our fantastic editor, Margaret McGuire, who first brought this idea to the table. Thank you also to Katie, Jane, Nicole, Eric, and the rest of the Quirk Books team for producing such a beautiful book.

We'd especially like to thank the wonderful folks who helped us test the many recipes in this book: Julie Deily, Taryn Collins, Jami Cowart, Sharon Hoffmann, Evi Dzieciolowski, Tripp Warren, Janet Kalandranis, Kaitlin Flannery, Kelly Lanza, Mackenzie Olson, Kristin Guy, Meghan Splawn, April Sutch, Julie Chiou, Melissa Cole, Kelly Randall, and Leah Short. We couldn't have done it without you!

Finally, thank you to our parents—who instilled in us a love of breakfast for dinner from an early age—for always supporting us in our crazy endeavors.

★ METRIC CONVERSION CHART ★

Use these rounded equivalents to convert between the traditional American systems used to measure volume and weight and the metric system.

VOLUME

American	Imperial	Metric
¼ teaspoon		1.25 milliliters
½ teaspoon		2.5 milliliters
1 teaspoon		5 milliliters
1 tablespoon		7.5 milliliters
¼ cup (4 tablespoons)	2 fluid ounces	15 milliliters
⅓ cup (5 tablespoons)	2½ fluid ounces	60 milliliters
½ cup (8 tablespoons)	4 fluid ounces	75 milliliters
⅔ cup (10 tablespoons)	5 fluid ounces	125 milliliters
¾ cup (12 tablespoons)	6 fluid ounces	150 milliliters
1 cup (16 tablespoons)	8 fluid ounces	175 milliliters
1¼ cups	10 fluid ounces	250 milliliters
1½ cups	12 fluid ounces	300 milliliters
1 pint (2 cups)	16 fluid ounces	350 milliliters

OVEN TEMPERATURES

	°F	°C	Gas Mark
Very cool	250–275	130–140	1/2–2
Cool	300	148	2
Warm	325	163	3
Medium	350	177	4
Medium hot	375–400	190–204	5–6
Hot	425	218	7
Very hot	450–500	232–245	8–9

WEIGHTS

American	Metric
¼ ounce	7 grams
½ ounce	15 grams
1 ounce	30 grams
2 ounces	55 grams
3 ounces	85 grams
4 ounces (¼ pound)	110 grams
5 ounces	140 grams
6 ounces	170 grams
7 ounces	200 grams
8 ounces (½ pound)	225 grams
9 ounces	250 grams
10 ounces	280 grams
11 ounces	310 grams
12 ounces (¾ pound)	340 grams
13 ounces	370 grams
14 ounces	400 grams
15 ounces	425 grams
16 ounces (1 pound)	450 grams

MEASUREMENTS

Pinch = $\frac{1}{16}$ teaspoon

$\frac{1}{2}$ tablespoon = $1\frac{1}{2}$ teaspoons

1 tablespoon = 3 teaspoons

$\frac{1}{4}$ cup = 4 tablespoons

$\frac{1}{3}$ cup = 5 tablespoons plus 1 teaspoon

$\frac{1}{2}$ cup = 8 tablespoons

$\frac{3}{4}$ cup = 12 tablespoons

1 cup = 16 tablespoons

1 quart = 4 cups

EQUIVALENCES

$\frac{1}{2}$ stick of butter = $\frac{1}{4}$ cup

1 stick of butter = $\frac{1}{2}$ cup

2 sticks of butter = 1 cup

2 large eggs = 3 small eggs

1 pound confectioner's sugar = $3\frac{3}{4}$ cups

INDEX

index
— 159 —